THE NEW CRITICAL IDIOM

SERIES EDITOR: JOHN DRAKAKIS, UNIVERSITY OF STIRLING

The New Critical Idiom is an invaluable series of introductory guides to today's critical terminology. Each book:

- provides a handy, explanatory guide to the use (and abuse) of the term
- offers an original and distinctive overview by a leading literary and cultural critic
- relates the term to the larger field of cultural representation.

With a strong emphasis on clarity, lively debate and the widest possible breadth of examples, *The New Critical Idiom* is an indispensable approach to key topics in literary studies.

Also available in this series:

THE AUTHOR

What is an 'author'? In this clearly structured introduction, Andrew Bennett discusses one of the most important critical and theoretical terms in literary studies. Examining the debates surrounding literary authorship, *The Author*:

- discusses Roland Barthes's controversial declaration of the 'death of the author'
- explores concepts of authority, ownership and originality
- traces changing definitions of the author and the historical development of authorship, from Homer to the present
- examines author theory in the context of debates on intentionality, feminism and historicism
- considers the significance of collaboration in literature and film
- analyses the importance of ideas of authorship for definitions of literature.

Accessible yet stimulating, this study offers the ideal introduction to a core notion in critical theory and is essential reading for all students of literature.

Andrew Bennett is Professor of English at the University of Bristol.

THE AUTHOR

Andrew Bennett

Routledge
Taylor & Francis Group

LONDON AND NEW YORK

First published 2005
by Routledge
2 Park Square, Milton Park, Abingdon, Oxon OX14 4RN

Simultaneously published in the USA and Canada
by Routledge
270 Madison Ave, New York, NY 10016

Routledge is an imprint of the Taylor & Francis Group

Transferred to Digital Printing 2009

Typeset in Adobe Garamond and Scala Sans by
Keystroke, Jacaranda Lodge, Wolverhampton

British Library Cataloguing in Publication Data
A catalogue record for this book is available from the British Library

Library of Congress Cataloging in Publication Data
Bennett, Andrew, 1960–
The author / Andrew Bennett.
p.   cm. – (The new critical idiom)
Includes bibliographical references and index.
1. Authorship–History. 2. Authorship–Philosophy. I. Title. II. Series.
PN145.B429 2005
808′.02′09–dc22
2004013734

ISBN 0–415–28163–6 (hbk)
ISBN 0–415–28164–4 (pbk)

CONTENTS

SERIES EDITOR'S PREFACE

The New Critical Idiom is a series of introductory books which seeks to extend the lexicon of literary terms, in order to address the radical changes which have taken place in the study of literature during the last decades of the twentieth century. The aim is to provide clear, well-illustrated accounts of the full range of terminology currently in use, and to evolve histories of its changing usage.

The current state of the discipline of literary studies is one where there is considerable debate concerning basic questions of terminology. This involves, among other things, the boundaries which distinguish the literary from the non-literary; the position of literature within the larger sphere of culture; the relationship between literatures of different cultures; and questions concerning the relation of literary to other cultural forms within the context of interdisciplinary studies.

It is clear that the field of literary criticism and theory is a dynamic and heterogeneous one. The present need is for individual volumes on terms which combine clarity of exposition with an adventurousness of perspective and a breadth of application. Each volume will contain as part of its apparatus some indication of the direction in which the definition of particular terms is likely to move, as well as expanding the disciplinary boundaries within which some of these terms have been traditionally contained. This will involve some re-situation of terms within the larger field of cultural representation, and will introduce examples from the area of film and the modern media in addition to examples from a variety of literary texts.

INTRODUCTION

SHAKESPEARE IN LOVE

> Who is that?
> Nobody – he's the author.

We can be fairly sure that this exchange about Shakespeare never took place, or at least that it only took place as part of the happily anachronistic Hollywood movie *Shakespeare in Love* (1998). It is unlikely that anyone said this because it is unlikely that anyone in 1593 (the year in which the film is set) would have spoken about Shakespeare or about any other poet or playwright as 'the author' in quite this way. Similarly, it is unlikely that any passionate lover of William Shakespeare, however passionate, however playful and however unsure of the poet's identity, would have asked him 'Are you the author of the plays of William Shakespeare?', as Viola does of Will in Peter Madden's film. It is unlikely that the word had quite the same resonance that it has for us, or that the knowing irony of these comments would have provoked quite the same reverence. A mark of the difference between our sense of the author and Shakespeare's is that in all the 880,000-odd words in his Complete Works this sense of 'the author' (as opposed to the more general sense of an authority or of one who is held responsible for something) appears just six times. In the 23,000-word script of *Shakespeare in Love* it is used seven times.

Shakespeare in Love is particularly concerned with authorship, with what it means to be an author, and especially of course with what it means to be that exemplary author, William Shakespeare. As the credits roll at the opening of the film, we momentarily view 'Will' privately trying out different versions of his signature: the film's title, inscribed in what we recognize as Shakespeare's handwriting, is superimposed over a sheet of paper covered with multiple variants of Will's handwritten name. Shakespeare, the film suggests, was as interested in the nature of his own name, of his own identity, and as interested in how that identity would be perceived, as we are. What is remarkable and what is successful about *Shakespeare in Love* is in fact its ability anachronistically to fuse this late twentieth-century sense of Shakespeare with a Shakespearean one. Indeed, Marc Norman and Tom Stoppard's script knowingly plays on this paradoxical figuration of Shakespeare as Shakespearean (paradoxical because Shakespeare is only Shakespearean after the event, in posterity, now). Many of the lines spoken by Will in *Shakespeare in Love* include words, phrases and even whole speeches from poems and plays written by (or at least ascribed to) the historical William Shakespeare. And one of the major themes of the movie reinforces the coincidence of life and work: the film revolves around the composition of a new Shakespeare play with the working title 'Romeo and Ethel the Pirate's Daughter', a play that is presented as intimately autobiographical, the star-crossed lovers being based on Shakespeare himself and his secret lover, Lady Viola. *Shakespeare in Love*, in other words, is as much about our own love affair with the figure or the idea of the author as it is about the poet, playwright and actor William Shakespeare, and it tells us as much about our own obsession with authorship as it does about Shakespeare himself or about his poems and plays. 'The search for an author', declares Marjorie Garber in the context of a discussion of Shakespeare's 'ghostly' presence in his plays and in our imaginations, 'like any other quest for parentage, reveals more about the searcher than about the sought' (Garber 1987: 27).

This book is about that intriguing figure, the author, that 'nobody' who holds for us such fascination. The book is, in part, about the distance between the idea of the author in Shakespeare's time and in our own. But it is also about the distance between 'nobody' and 'the author'; between naming and anonymity; between the presence and absence or life and death of the author.

WHAT IS AN AUTHOR?

William Wordsworth's Preface to the 1800 edition of the *Lyrical Ballads* was written as a defence of the poems collected in those two revolutionary, influential and idiosyncratic volumes of verse (first published anonymously as one much shorter volume of poems written by Wordsworth and Samuel Taylor Coleridge in 1798). In order to defend the poems from what had already seemed to him a hasty and unjust reception, Wordsworth felt obliged to write an extended analysis of the nature of poetry when he revised the Preface in 1802: he needed, he decided, to define poetry itself. But in order to do this he was impelled in turn to ask a prior question: 'Taking up the subject, then, upon general grounds', he says, 'I ask what is meant by the word Poet? What is a Poet?' (Wordsworth 1984: 603). Wordsworth's answer to the question, interesting as it is in itself, is perhaps less significant than the fact that the question was posed. Fifteen years later, Wordsworth's critical manoeuvre will be repeated and reinforced by Coleridge, in his *Biographia Literaria* (1817): 'What is poetry? is so nearly the same question with, what is a poet?', declares Coleridge, 'that the answer to the one is involved in the solution of the other' (Coleridge 1983: 2:15). While the question is not new in the early nineteenth century, there does seem to be a new urgency in the asking of it. For Sir Philip Sidney, writing two centuries earlier, the question 'What is a poet?' is less troubling since the Romans and ancient Greeks have already given us an answer: the Romans called the poet *vates*, Sidney tells us, 'a diviner, foreseer, or prophet', and the Greeks gave us the word 'poet', from *poiein*, 'to make' (Sidney 2002: 83–4). The difficulty that Wordsworth and Coleridge have in answering the question, the fact that they don't rest content with received opinion, suggests that the question of authorship is for them itself critical. It is a question, in fact, that marks a crisis in literary culture. Moreover, while Sidney is interested most of all in what a poet *does* (see Rose 1993: 13), Wordsworth and Coleridge are interested in who he or she *is*. As I shall try to show in Chapter 3, below, the questioning of the nature of authorship in Romantic poetics marks a turning point in the history of the institution of literature. It marks a turn in poetics and literary theory away from a focus on the literary work towards the subject who makes or creates the work, towards the poet or author as a site of analysis and exploration. As

Charles Taylor comments, Wordsworth and Coleridge are at the same time reflecting a long history of thinking about artistic activity and marking a culmination in that tradition, a tradition which 'makes us admire the artist and the creator more than any other civilization ever has' and that 'convinces us that a life spent in artistic creation or performance is eminently worthwhile' (Taylor 1989: 22). And it is a tradition that has given us the sense of the 'superb and solitary romantic figure of the sovereign author', as Roger Chartier puts it, one whose 'primary or final intention contains *the* meaning of the work and whose biography commands its writing with transparent immediacy' (Chartier 1994: 28).

This book focuses on the question that Wordsworth raises: 'What is meant by the word Poet? What is a Poet?' And it extends the honorific word 'poet' (as Wordsworth effectively does) to include all of those engaged in the production of literary texts, to include 'authors' in general: 'What is meant by the word Author?', we might ask with Michel Foucault, 'What is an Author?' (Foucault 1979). The history of literary criticism from the earliest times may in fact be said to be organized around conceptions of authorship: as the theorist of authorship Séan Burke comments, 'there is no theory of literature or the text which does not imply a certain stance' towards the author (Burke 1995: ix). Debates over authorship have been particularly intense in criticism and theory during the last two centuries, and especially over the last fifty years. Literary theory, we might say, is largely a question of author theory.

Nevertheless, recent discussions of authorship may be reduced, quite crudely, to two different kinds of concern, both of which are central to any discussion of literature, to any reading of literary texts, and to any elaboration of literary theory. On the one hand there is a series of problems to do with interpretation, with critical understanding, with literary evaluation and intention: these are problems centring on the issue characterized most famously in the title of W.K. Wimsatt and Monroe C. Beardsley's 1946 essay 'The Intentional Fallacy', and involving the question of whether an author means what she says, and whether we should be concerned with what she thinks she means in the first place. Roland Barthes's essay 'The Death of the Author' (1967) is perhaps the most striking and certainly the most influential expression of anti-intentionalism, provocatively asserting that 'We know now' that a text does not contain 'a single "theological" meaning (the "message" of the

Author-God)' and declaring that once the author has been 'removed', 'the claim to decipher a text becomes quite futile' (Barthes 1995: 128). On the other hand, there is a more historically, socially and institutionally involved set of issues surrounding authorship and authority to which Barthes's essay also alludes. These involve Foucault's notion of the 'author-function' and more generally what we might call the 'praxis' or 'pragmatics' of authorship: the social, historical, institutional and discursive limits on, and conventions of, the author. In this context, theorists and historians of authorship have attended to its multiple and changing representations in historically specific sites and articulations; they have considered the effects of publishing technologies, practices and institutions, and the history of copyright law and censorship on conceptions of authorship; they have analysed the nature of collaborative authorship and its effect on the understanding of literary texts; they have investigated the significance of gender, ethnic, class or racial identifications and identities for the structure and understanding of authorship and authority; and they have explored the relationship of authorship to questions of intertextuality and plagiarism, parody and forgery, to representations of the self and autobiography, to pseudonymity, and anonymity, and more generally to the institution of literature itself.

This book begins with a discussion of the two most influential essays on authorship in twentieth-century criticism, Barthes's 'The Death of the Author' and Foucault's 'What is an Author?' (1969). In many respects, these essays have dominated discussions of authorship during the decades since their first publication: they have largely set the terms of the debate and have in equal measure been applauded for their radical reinterpretation of authorship and criticized for their alleged incoherence, inaccuracies and anachronisms. Chapter 2 examines recent attempts to understand the literary and cultural contexts of the development of the concept of authorship and offers a brief survey of issues surrounding the history of authorship before the institution of the so-called 'Romantic author'. Chapter 3 concerns the conflicted and paradoxical representation of authorship in the Romantic period, the period that may be said to have fully instituted the modern sense and the modern privileging of the author as autonomous, original, and expressive. Chapter 4 returns to more recent critical and theoretical debates and suggests that the major critical and theoretical movements of the twentieth century, including formalism and new criticism, feminism and new historicism, are bound up with questions of authorship, and indeed bound up with such questions even as they distance themselves from issues of intentionality and subjectivity. Chapter 5 discusses collaboration in literature and film, a practice that may seem to challenge our sense of authorship as autonomous and as originating in a single, unique individual. Chapter 6 addresses recent critical and theoretical discourses to look at ways in which the question of authorship, pervasive as it is in contemporary criticism and culture more generally, is involved in the very institution of literature itself. The book ends with an appendix, an 'Author Lexicon', comprising a checklist of terms that critics have used to denote authors or author-figures, a list that might help to indicate the intricate strategies of definition that critics and theorists have been compelled to develop in their attempts to bring some order to the field of author theory.

THE AUTHOR, sb.

There is, of course, a history of authorship. The *Oxford English Dictionary* records that the word 'author' comes from the Latin verb *augere*, 'to make to grow, originate, promote, increase', which developed into the words *auctor* and *auctoritas* in the medieval period, with their sense of authority, their sense of the *auctor* as one of the ancient writers who could be called upon to guarantee an argument's validity. The dictionary defines the familiar contemporary sense of the author as 'One who sets forth written statements; the composer or writer of a treatise or book' (*OED*, author, sb.3a), a definition which is associated with a more general sense of someone who 'originates or gives existence to anything: a. An inventor, constructor, or founder . . . b. (*of all, of nature, of the universe*, etc) The Creator' (*OED*, author, sb.1). The *OED* also informs us that both of these senses enter the language in Chaucer's time, at the end of the fourteenth century, as *auctor, auctour*, and later *aucthour* and *authour*. Furthermore, it identifies the author with 'authority', as a person 'on whose authority a statement is made; an authority, an informant' (sb.4), and as someone who has 'authority over others; a director, ruler, commander' (sb.5). Finally, the dictionary lists the largely obsolete but still important sense of an author as 'One who begets; a father, an ancestor' (sb.2). As we shall see, the modern sense of the author develops rapidly in the eighteenth century, and the *OED* also reflects this in listing a spate of words which all enter the English language at that time: 'authorial' (first entry 1796), 'authoring' (1742), 'authorism' ('The position or character of a writer of books'; 1761), 'authorless' (1713), 'authorling' ('a petty author; an insignificant writer'; 1771), 'authorly' ('proper to authors'; 1784), and 'authorship' ('occupation or career as a writer of books'; 1710).

Despite the historical and conceptual complexities of the idea of the author and despite the voluminous critical attention paid to it, there is nevertheless a basic or what might now seem to be a 'common-sense' conception of authorship, of the 'modern' or post-medieval author at least, against which other perhaps more sophisticated and certainly more historically nuanced senses work. The *OED*'s entry for 'author' suggests that this common-sense notion of the author involves the idea of an individual (singular) who is responsible for or who originates, who writes or composes, a (literary) text and who is thereby considered an inventor or founder and who is associated with the inventor or founder of all of nature, with God (with God-the-father), and is thought to have certain ownership rights over the text as well as a certain authority over its interpretation. The author is able to influence others and is often thought of as having authority over matters of opinion, as being one to be trusted, even obeyed. This is what the historian of authorship Martha Woodmansee refers to as the 'contemporary usage' of the word 'author', a usage which denotes 'an individual who is solely responsible – and thus exclusively deserving of credit – for the production of a unique, original work' (Woodmansee 1994a: 35). This sense of authorship, of the author as possessing and expressing a 'sovereign solitude' (Derrida 1978: 226), is closely allied to the idea of genius, an idea which is itself reinvented and reinvigorated in eighteenth-century European culture. For Wordsworth and others, Woodmansee suggests, 'the genius is someone who does something utterly new, unprecedented', someone who 'produces something that never existed before' (Woodmansee 1994a: 39). In particular, of course, this power of the author, his or her authority, concerns the uses to which a text is put, the way that it is interpreted. Embedded within this 'Romantic' or 'modern' sense of authorship is an implicit assumption that the author of a work is in control of that work, knows what it means and intends something by it, that she delimits and defines its interpretations. Indeed, in this sense of authorship the author *guarantees* the meaning(s) of the text since she was present to herself as she wrote or composed it and was fully conscious of and knowledgeable about her words, meanings and intentions. Such an idea of the author presupposes that the author is not subject to the 'external' forces of history, society, the law, and politics that after Marx we call 'ideology'; and not subject to the kinds of 'internal' forces, drives, desires, impulses, that, after Freud, we know as the 'unconscious'. Working against this sense of authorship, then, are some of the most powerful explanatory discourses of our, of contemporary, culture. Challenging the idea of authorship as authoritative and controlling are those views of the individual or the 'subject' as precisely lacking in agency, as *controlled* by ideology, as split or divided by the unconscious, and even as subject to, or the subject of, language itself. Indeed, we might conclude that the question of this authorial conflict of agency and its absence, deterioration, or eradication is a major part of our fascination with literary texts. Many of the debates over the author in contemporary literary theory involve disagreements over the nature of the human subject, about notions of subjectivity and agency and about what it means to be human. But such debates are also, in the end, about what we mean when we talk about 'literature', what it is that we are responding to as we read a poem or a novel, and why it is, finally, that we read literary texts at all.

1

THE 'DEATH' OF THE AUTHOR

'Those who say the author is dead', quips the Australian poet Les Murray, 'usually have it in mind to rifle his wardrobe' (quoted in Crawford 2001: 15). Roland Barthes died in 1980, some thirteen years after declaring the author to be dead in 'The Death of the Author' (1967), and the wardrobe of his essay has been rifled ever since. Indeed, some would argue, extending and deforming Murray's metaphor, that this author, Roland Barthes, this ruler of the empire of signs, was an emperor with no clothes. And yet his essay has done much to energize discussions of authorship in the decades since its first publication. In fact, Barthes's announcement of the death of the author has had the effect of bringing to the fore the question of the author in literary criticism and theory. In what might seem to be a perverse confirmation of Barthes's argument, the influence of his essay has in some ways been in direct conflict with his apparent intention.

In the decades after its first publication in 1967,* Barthes's essay was often taken as the last word on the author. The essay was often conceived

---

* A common misconception concerning Barthes's essay is that it made its first appearance in 1968. The essay is even presented as such, in a perhaps understandable gesture of linguistic chauvinism, in the scholarly French edition of Barthes's collected works (Barthes 1993–5: 2.491–5). In fact, though, Barthes's

of in terms of a theorist reading the last rites over the corpse of the idea of the author. And such an understanding often went no further than the 'stark extremity', as Michael North calls it, of the essay's title (North 2001: 1377). The polemical aggression embedded within the phrase prompted a sense that Barthes was issuing a death-threat or indeed that he was engaged in an assassination attempt. Indeed, Barthes's title was often taken synecdochically to stand for the whole iconoclastic project of poststructuralism, to which his work was increasingly allied. 'Post-structuralism', which involves, in this context, a radical scepticism towards the integrity of a subject's thoughts, meanings and intentions, or of a subject's ownership of those thoughts, meanings and intentions, was often interpreted as an assertion of 'the death of the author'. And the weaknesses of Barthes's essay, including its tendency towards unfounded generalizations, its neglect of academic or scholarly precision, and its wayward way with literary history, were often seen as the weaknesses of the project of poststructuralism itself.

There is, in fact, a reasonably straightforward sense in which Barthes's declaration may seem to be relatively uncontroversial. One of the fundamental differences between speech and writing is that, unlike speech, writing *remains*, that it lasts after the person that writes has departed. This is a distinction that Plato commented on in the *Phaedrus* in the fourth century BC, that came to prominence again with the publication of Jacques Derrida's *Of Grammatology* in the same year as that of Barthes's essay, and that is also recognized by a more conventional theorist of writing such as David Olson (see Plato 2001c; Derrida 1976; Olson 1994: xv). In other words, unlike acts of speech, acts of writing can be read after the absence, including the radical absence that constitutes death, of its author. You can read this sentence now, in the 'now' of your reading, whether or not I am alive. In principle, writing operates in the same way in either case: *structural*

essay was presented at a seminar in 1967 and first published in English in the United States in the Autumn–Winter 1967 number of *Aspen* magazine (vol. 5–6). It was subsequently published in French in *Mantéia* 5:4 (1968), and collected in English in *Image, Music, Text* (1977), and in French in *Le Bruissement de la langue* (1984). The essay is now very widely available, having been endlessly reprinted in English in such anthologies as Caughie 1981, Rice and Waugh 1996, Burke 1995, Leitch 2001, Irwin 2002a, and Finkelstein and McCleery 2002.

to writing is the possibility of the absence, including the death, of the subject who writes. By contrast, at least until Thomas Edison's invention of the phonograph in 1877, the act of speaking necessarily involved the presence of the speaker. And even Edison's invention made little difference to this principle, since the phonograph, the gramophone, the digital voice recorder and any other device that transmits or makes a copy of your voice is essentially a writing ('-graph', 'gramo-') rather than a speaking instrument. On one level at least, then, the assertion of the 'death of the author' may be seen as giving no more than proper recognition to the nature of writing and to its difference from speech.

But for Barthes the consequences of this recognition of the author's absence in principle are wide-ranging, and much is at stake in his essay, in Barthes's declaration of radical textuality, of texts working independently of their authors. Barthes raises fundamental questions of literary interpretation and 'appreciation'; he interrogates the nature of literary speech acts and of literary-critical judgements; he attempts to reconfigure our understanding of how texts work; he subverts long-held beliefs concerning the priority of the human, of individuality, of subjectivity and subjective experience; and he challenges conventional notions of biography and autobiography as well as traditional conceptions of the institution of literature and the nature and status of the literary work. In this chapter, I will try to account for the importance and significance of Barthes's essay before moving on to consider Michel Foucault's influential response to and development of his position in 'What is an Author?', an essay that may be said to re-open literary theory to questions of authorship and open authorship to the question of history. Barthes's and Foucault's essays constitute the founding statements of much subsequent critical and theoretical work on the author: almost forty years later we are still caught up in debates about the problem of authorship instigated by Barthes and Foucault in the late 1960s.

WHO SPEAKS?

Properly to assess Barthes's argument about the author one would in fact need to engage not just with a single title or even a single essay but with at least three overlapping essays from the late 1960s and early 1970s – 'The Death of the Author' itself, 'From Work to Text' (1971) and 'Theory of the Text' (1973) – as well as with a number of Barthes's books, including *S/Z* (1970) and *The Pleasure of the Text* (1973). But one would also need to engage with a wider cultural and intellectual context, a wider textuality and politics. In keeping with his emphasis on intertextuality, according to which a text is no more than a 'tissue of . . . citations' from multiple other texts (Barthes 1981: 39), and in keeping with a new, decentred sense of subjectivity and of textuality, Barthes remarks at the end of 'From Work to Text' that he has 'in many respects only recapitulated what is being developed around me' (Barthes 1979: 81). In this regard, an understanding of 'The Death of the Author' involves an understanding of some of the major mid-century philosophical and ideological critiques of liberalism and humanism. Nevertheless, I will try to focus quite closely in this discussion on Barthes's most famous, most polemical statement, 'The Death of the Author'.

Barthes begins his essay by asking us to consider a sentence from Balzac's short story *Sarrasine*, itself the subject of his next book, *S/Z*, an extraordinary meditation on the multiple 'codes' of Balzac's short story. The sentence involves a description of the protagonist of *Sarrasine*, a castrated man disguised as a woman: 'This was woman herself, with her sudden fears, her irrational whims, her instinctive worries, her impetuous boldness, her fussings, and her delicious sensibility' (quoted in Barthes 1995: 125). 'Who is speaking thus?', Barthes asks. His answer is that we cannot know who speaks. The sentence, he suggests, could be spoken by the castrato himself, by Balzac the individual, by Balzac as an author 'professing "literary" ideas', by 'universal wisdom', or by an idea of a person proposed by 'Romantic psychology'. We cannot know who speaks, Barthes argues, indeed we will never know, because writing involves the 'destruction of every voice, of every point of origin' (p. 125). Barthes agrees with Stéphane Mallarmé's declaration that the literary work, the 'pure work', involves 'the disappearance of the poet's voice' (quoted in Nesbit 1987: 230). Barthes's opening salvo in 'The Death of the Author', then, abolishes authorial voice, eliminates voice as origin and source, voice as identity, unity, as what Foucault will call the 'principle of a certain unity in writing' (Foucault 1979: 151). 'It is language which speaks', Barthes declares, 'not the author' (Barthes 1995: 126).

There are in fact other, more conventional ways in which Balzac's sentence might be interpreted, ways in which its origin might be specified.

It could, for example, be read within a framework of a conventional distribution between the narrator and what Wayne Booth calls the 'implied author' (where the 'implied author' is the image or idea of the author suggested by the text, a more traditional way of talking about the author that avoids presuming beyond the text to an historical agent). Or one could consider the ways in which Balzac exploits the common nineteenth-century realist mode of 'free indirect discourse', whereby, through a kind of literary ventriloquism, a so-called 'omniscient' narrator speaks with a character's words or from his or her perspective, making it impossible to pinpoint the precise location of narrator, author and character. But such strategies for explaining the origin, the 'voice' of Balzac's sentence ultimately rely on an idea of Balzac himself, on authorial agency and control, on the idea that a text is ordered and directed by a certain unified, unique and singular subjectivity, by the mind or consciousness of Honoré de Balzac. Barthes, by contrast, suggests that writing radically subverts our sense of a stable voice, of a stable origin, for speech or language. He suggests that the instability or uncertainty of the source, of the voice, in Balzac's novel involves the radical disappearance, indeed the radical non-appearance, of the author. Barthes uses Balzac's sentence to argue that writing is fundamentally without origin. In doing so, he seeks to move authority away from the author, the author as source of the work, the fount of all knowledge and meaning, towards the system of language, the textual codes that produce effects of meaning: for Barthes, language speaks, not the author.

A REVOLUTIONARY POETICS

Barthes's essay constituted a revolutionary critique of conventional conceptions of authorship and interpretation, part of the 'veritable revolution' of structuralism and poststructuralism (Couturier 1995: 13). But it was also part of a more general critique of authority itself: what is at stake is 'the subversion not just of the ideology of authorship but of authority in all its forms' (Moriarty 1991: 101). The essay was first published in an avant-garde, iconoclastic and formally experimental US magazine, *Aspen*, which in fact consisted of a box containing twenty-eight artefacts, including movies, records, diagrams, cardboard cut-outs, as well as more conventional texts. The issue was dedicated to Stéphane Mallarmé and included work by, amongst others, Marcel Duchamp, Alain Robbe-Grillet, Michel Butor, Merce Cunningham, Samuel Beckett and John Cage. The collection as a whole and Barthes's essay in particular were aimed at confronting and subverting conventional ways of thinking about, of approaching or theorizing, literature and art, particularly with respect to conventional oppositions of 'high' art to low cultural values (see Nesbit 1987: 240–4; Burke 1998: 211; North 2001: 1378). And Barthes's essay was written from within the context of Marxist, psychoanalytical, structuralist and poststructuralist transformations and deformations in philosophy, linguistics, anthropology and literary and cultural studies of late-1960s French intellectual culture. If the essay was written in 1967 and not, as has so often been assumed and sometimes even asserted, 'at the height of the antiestablishment uprisings of May 1968' (Leitch 2001: 1458), it is easy to see why this connection might be made. This indeed is revolution in the head.

Barthes is concerned to challenge, to destabilize and undermine what he sees as the oppressive, controlling, authority-figure of the author, 'that somewhat decrepit deity of the old criticism', as Barthes refers to it in S/Z (Barthes 1974: 211). He is concerned to subvert the power-structures embedded within the promotion of such a figure, within conventional accounts of authorship, textuality and the literary institution. For Barthes, the idea of the author is a 'tyranny' demanding a quasi-theological approach to reading and interpretation in which the text's single, stable and definable meaning is understood to be underwritten by the author, by the author as a kind of presiding deity, by the 'Author-God'. Even Barthes's title itself, an allusion to Friedrich Nietzsche's late nineteenth-century declaration of the 'death of God', links authorialism with theism. 'To give a text an Author', Barthes momentously declares, 'is to impose a limit on that text, to furnish it with a final signified, to close the writing' (Barthes 1995: 128–9). The traditional conception of authorship involves a sense that, as Barthes remarks in S/Z, 'the author is a god' whose 'place of origin' is the text's signified or meaning. The critic, according to this logic, acts like a priest, with the task of 'deciphering the Writing of the god' (Barthes 1974: 174).

The idea of the author in the sense that Barthes is attacking involves a particular strategy of reading, it involves a sense that the text originates in and is therefore defined by and limited to the subjectivity, the mind, the consciousness, the intentions, the psychology and the life of the individual author. The author, in this model, not only 'owns' the text but owns, guarantees, originates, its meanings, its interpretations. The logic of this understanding of authorship entails a strictly defined role for the critic. The critic is at once fundamentally limited, fundamentally constrained, and at the same time the arbiter of a text's proper interpretation, of its meaning. In other words, the critic is, on the one hand, limited by her sense of the author's intentions, ideas, consciousness. The author is seen as asserting a god-like power, a power of omniscience and omnipotence over the text's meanings. Meaning is 'univocal', limited to the sense authorized by the author. But on the other hand Barthes also sees this apparent limitation as a strategy of critical empowerment and aggrandizement, since the critic can now become the true judge of the text's meaning, the guardian of authorial intention. The critic's task is to identify the 'Author' (capital 'A') or, as Barthes says, 'its hypostases society, history, psyché, liberty'. Once the critic performs this revelation, interpretation and the text are at an end: 'victory to the critic' (p. 129).

By redescribing the 'modern' author as 'scriptor' and displacing meaning from author to text, Barthes is able to argue that readers will be liberated from the oppressive control of authorial consciousness and critical guardianship. Authors, as K.K. Ruthven puts it, are 'legal personages who both pre-exist and survive the texts they produce', by contrast with 'scriptors', who are 'wholly coterminous with the texts that engender them' (Ruthven 2001: 112). Rather than a controlling consciousness, the scriptor is an agent of language. By using this term, the focus of the theorist's interest can shift from attempting to understand the author's intentions or the way that her life, thought or consciousness defines and limits the text's meaning, to a certain thinking of textuality, of textuality without origin. The text is now understood as the site of a 'plurality of meaning', of '*irreducible* plurality' (Barthes 1979: 76). For Barthes, the modern text is a 'multi-dimensional space in which a variety of writings, none of them original, blend and clash'. Rather than a document with a single source and a single interpretation, this text is constituted as a 'tissue of quotations drawn from the innumerable centres of culture' (Barthes 1995: 128). Barthes's text is intertextual. But this idea embraces a new conception of intertextuality that goes beyond specific and identifiable echoes, allusions, or references. Barthes's is a radical intertextuality without origin. As he comments, in 'Theory of the Text', in an important recapitulation and rephrasing of 'The Death of the Author', a text is 'a new tissue of past citations' (Barthes 1981: 39). But these 'citations' by which the text is constituted are 'anonymous formulae whose origin can scarcely ever be located', they are 'unconscious or automatic quotations, given without quotation-marks' (p. 39). For Barthes, intertextual citationality is 'anonymous, irrecoverable' (Barthes 1979: 72). Such a model of textuality – textuality as intertextuality – eliminates the central, controlling power of authorial consciousness. The author is replaced by a decentred system of language, language as machine, as 'dialogue, parody, contestation . . . multiplicity' (Barthes 1995: 129).

THE TYRANNY OF THE AUTHOR

While Barthes's essay is often conceived of as articulating a general philosophical or literary-theoretical position, it also in fact involves a certain thinking, briefly alluded to, of literary history, of the historicity of authorship. In the first place, indeed, it involves the proposition that the idea of the author is historical, that the author is a historical figure, but one who has had his day and who is now dead. But it also involves a claim about the invention of authorship at a certain point in the cultural history of the West, of Europe. It is this historicity of authorship that Michel Foucault will develop more fully in 'What is an Author?' and that we will examine in more detail in Chapter 2, below. For Barthes, the author is a 'modern figure' that emerges out of the Middle Ages, with 'English empiricism, French rationalism and the personal faith of the Reformation', and it is bound up with the more general 'ideology' of capitalism (Barthes 1995: 125–6). Since capitalism is intellectually and ideologically grounded in the autonomy and self-fulfilment of the humanist conception of the individual, the ascription of meaning to the author can be seen as part of a wider historical privileging of subjectivity. As the Marxist theorist Pierre Macherey had confidently declared in *A Theory of Literary Production* (1966), 'The proposition that the writer or artist is a creator belongs to a humanist ideology' (Macherey 1995: 230). Barthes argues that the 'modernist' aesthetic, developed in the late nineteenth and twentieth centuries, offers a model of the text that resists the capitalist insistence on individuality and therefore on the 'tyranny' of the author. He gives as examples (in what Seán Burke has called a 'palpably false' lineage (Burke 1998: 8)) the work of Stéphane Mallarmé (whose 'entire poetics consists in suppressing the author in the interests of writing'), Paul Valéry (who 'never stopped calling into question and deriding the Author'), and Marcel Proust (whose massive psychological and autobiographical novel was in fact directed towards 'inexorably blurring, by an extreme subtilization, the relation between the writer and his characters') (Barthes 1995: 126). Barthes's essay is in fact torn between his wishful thinking with regard to the joyful possibility that we have overcome this ideology, that the oppressive figure of the author has been superseded by the textualism of avant-garde writing, and his obvious dismay that this is not in fact the case, that the modernist aesthetic remains a relatively marginalized one in contemporary culture (see Lamarque 2002: 83).

In his announcement of the death of the author, therefore, Barthes may be understood to be both describing an historical event, an historical moment, and at the same time mounting a polemic, a provocation against the contemporary privileging of the individual, against the 'prestige' of the 'human person' (Barthes 1995: 126). In this sense, the essay is therefore carefully duplicitous. While its title and its polemical thrust assert that the author has passed away, that the figure of the author is now outdated, superseded by the text itself, at the same time Barthes makes it clear that the author still holds sway, still asserts a 'tyrannous' hold on readers' imaginations:

> The *author* still reigns in histories of literature, biographies of writers, interviews, magazines, as in the very consciousness of men of letters anxious to unite their person and their work through diaries and memoirs. The image of literature to be found in ordinary culture is tyrannically centred on the author, his person, his life, his tastes, his passions, while criticism still consists for the most part in saying that Baudelaire's work is the failure of Baudelaire the man, Van Gogh's his madness, Tchaikovsky's his vice. The *explanation* of a work is always sought in the man or woman who produced it, as if it were always in the end, through the more or less transparent allegory of the fiction, the voice of a single person, the *author* 'confiding' in us.

(p. 126)

Barthes's declaration of the death of the author is not only a description of what has happened but also an argument about what *ought to happen*. Barthes is concerned to explore a literary-historical development, a historical change in the conception and representation of authorship, its 'disappearance' in the work of certain modernist or avant-garde writers, whose work resists the 'capitalist' hegemony of authorcentric, bourgeois, humanist ideology. But he is also concerned to argue that such writers in fact expose what needs to be recognized as the truth of authorship, that they reveal the author to be constituted by textuality itself, to be an effect of the text.

THE BIRTH OF THE READER

In the end, Barthes's decentring of authorship, his model of authorial absence or dissolution or death, itself relies on a certain centre. For in one of the essay's most controversial and problematic moves, Barthes ends 'The Death of the Author' by arguing that 'a text's unity lies not in its origin but in its destination'. In this gesture, Barthes replaces the controlling, limiting subjectivity of the author with the controlling, limiting subjectivity of the reader – albeit an anonymous reader, 'simply that *someone* who holds together in a single field all the traces by which the written text is constituted' (p. 129). Thus the essay ends with another memorable and influential but nevertheless highly questionable, indeed mystificatory, declaration: 'the birth of the reader must be at the cost of the death of the Author' (p. 130). In this sense, Barthes's radical subversion of authority, his project of textual liberation, is exposed at the end of 'The Death of the Author' to the stringency of a certain circumscription, a certain subjectivity, as one model of unity and essentialism centred around the figure of the author is replaced by another, centred around the figure of the reader. More importantly, perhaps, Barthes's call-to-arms for a revolution in both literature and criticism embeds within itself its own contradiction or its own circularity. Since reading itself may be said to involve, even in Barthes's own description, the construction of a 'unity', a 'unity' which can be no other than the (desire for an) author, Barthes's famous slogan might be concluded by saying that 'the birth of the reader must be at the cost of the death of the author' who nevertheless lives on in the life (the desire, the imagination) of that reader. And as if in confirmation of the reader's authorial desires, after his declaration of the death of the author Barthes never seemed to stop contemplating the *life* of the author, whether in 'autobiographical' works such as *Roland Barthes by Roland Barthes* (1975), *A Lover's Discourse* (1977), and *Camera Lucida* (1980), or in the comment in *Sade, Fourier, Loyola* (1971) that 'the pleasure of the Text also includes the amicable return of the author', although now the author 'has no unity', is 'a mere plural of "charms", the site of a few tenuous details' (Barthes 1977a: 8–9). As Barthes comments in *The Pleasure of the Text*, while the author as 'institution' is 'dead', while his 'civil status' and 'biographical person' have lost the powerful 'paternity' over his work that they once had, nevertheless, 'in the text, in a way, *I desire* the author: I need his figure . . . as he needs mine' (Barthes 1975: 27).

WHAT DOES IT MATTER WHO IS SPEAKING?

As we have seen, Barthes opens his 1967 essay by questioning the origin of voice in a Balzac short story: 'who is speaking thus?' Towards the beginning of his 1969 essay 'What is an Author?', Michel Foucault echoes this questioning and responds with another question, a question that, rather than originating with Foucault or indeed with Barthes, originates in a text by Samuel Beckett. Foucault quotes Beckett's *Texts for Nothing*: '"What does it matter who is speaking", someone said, "what does it matter who is speaking"' (Foucault 1979: 141). While Barthes asks who is speaking, and answers that nobody is speaking or that writing originates only in an infinitely dispersed textuality, Foucault emphasizes the significance of the question itself. In answer to the question 'who is speaking?', there is another question, 'what does it *matter* who is speaking?' Foucault's answer is that, in fact, it matters very much who speaks, or who we think is speaking, and his essay is largely constituted by an attempt to explore the consequences of this mattering. At the same time, his essay, like Barthes's, involves a yearning towards a future in which our only response to such a question would be a shrug or, as Foucault puts it, at the close of the essay, a 'stirring of an indifference' (Foucault 1979: 160). Foucault wants it to matter not at all who is speaking.

While nowhere explicitly citing or referring to Barthes's essay, nor indeed directly engaging with or challenging Barthes's pronouncements,

Foucault's essay is nevertheless heavily indebted, pervasively and ago-nistically influenced by that precursor text (as well as, again implicitly, by the work of Jacques Derrida). Barthes's essay may be said to be Foucault's unstated premise, his silent progenitor and antagonist, his 'intertext'. But instead of confronting Barthes, Foucault transposes his arguments. While Barthes defines writing, for example, as 'that neutral, composite, oblique space where our subject slips away, the negative where all identity is lost' (Barthes 1995: 125), Foucault transforms this position by arguing that writing creates 'a space into which the writing subject constantly disappears' (Foucault 1979: 142). This apparently minor difference is in fact fundamental and exemplifies the distinction between Barthes's zestful polemic (of approximately 2,500 words, in seven disjointed paragraphs) and Foucault's more carefully argued and more historically decisive but still polemical, still somewhat fragmentary and at times infuriatingly opaque essay (of approximately 8,500 words, in 51 paragraphs and 5 sections). For Barthes, writing is a negative space into which the subject 'slips away' and where 'all identity is lost'. For Foucault, by contrast, the disappearance of the writing subject is a continuous process, one that itself requires analysis. Barthes is concerned only with a certain absence, a 'negative' space of writing. Foucault is concerned with the social and historical construction of a 'writing subject' and posits writing as a space in which this disappearing is endlessly enacted:

> It is not enough [Foucault declares] . . . to repeat the empty affirmation that the author has disappeared. For the same reason, it is not enough to keep repeating (after Nietzsche) that God and man have died a common death. Instead, we must locate the space left empty by the author's disappearance, follow the distribution of gaps and breaches, and watch for the openings that this disappearance uncovers.
>
> (Foucault 1979: 145)

It is important, then, that Barthes is both present as an antagonist in Foucault's essay and at the same time absent, unacknowledged, since his eerie status within the essay bears out or performs Foucault's sense of the author as ceaselessly disappearing, as constituted by the enactment of a certain abstraction. Barthes is an apparition and this phantasmatic status of Barthes's essay within Foucault's may also be said to enact, and in a sense to confirm, Barthes's own declaration that his work is no more than a 'recapitulation' of work that 'is being developed around me'. Thus when he directly addresses the notion of the 'death of the author' and suggests that it is an idea that was recognized 'some time ago', Foucault makes it ambiguously clear that Barthes both is and is not the origin, that he both is and is not the antagonist.

Like Barthes, Foucault is concerned to analyse contemporary writing as that which goes beyond the 'dimension of expression', beyond the conception of writing as the expression of a certain subjectivity, the expression of an individual who is outside of or who precedes the text. Foucault is concerned above all with the poststructuralists' notion of the 'effacement of the writing subject's individual characteristics' (Foucault 1979: 142). And yet he is also rightly suspicious of the Barthesian notion of the 'death of the author', sensing the danger that arguments designed to challenge an author's privileged position will in fact tend to work to preserve that privilege and, as he puts it, 'suppress the real meaning' of the author's disappearance (p. 143). The danger is that just as there can be no concept of the *oeuvre* without an organizing authorial origin, the formalizing appeal to the *work* itself, to the work in itself, depends on the individual author's unifying presence: in this respect, the Barthesian notion of writing, of *écriture*, itself also 'subtly preserve[s]' the author, simply transposing 'the empirical characteristics of the author into a transcendental anonymity' (p. 144). God-like, the author becomes, precisely in his absence, the fount, the origin of all meaning. The point is illustrated by Stephen Daedalus's modernist and aestheticist, indeed Flaubertian, declaration of the author's impersonality in James Joyce's *A Portrait of the Artist as a Young Man* (1914–15). The 'personality of the artist . . . finally refines itself out of existence, impersonalises itself', Stephen proposes. Like the 'God of the creation', he argues, the artist 'remains within or behind or beyond or above his handiwork, invisible, refined out of existence, indifferent, paring his fingernails' (Joyce 2000: 180–1). As this famous declaration makes clear, the absence of the author involves another, more pervasive presence: the artist or author is 'within or behind or beyond or above' the artwork, invisible but omnipresent, the source 'behind' the text. Like Barthes's anti-theological polemic, in other words, Stephen's Joycean declaration of authorial absence serves to construct the author as a kind of omniscient, theological figure.

THE AUTHOR-FUNCTION

Foucault's project, then, is not to repeat the often repeated assertion, since Mallarmé, or since Flaubert or Joyce, of the 'impersonality' or the disappearance of the author, but rather to 'follow the distribution of gaps and breaks, and watch for the openings' that the disappearance of the author reveals (Foucault 1979: 145). In this respect, 'What is an Author?' is dedicated to analysing the operation of what Foucault calls the 'author-function', the naming of which may itself be said to be his most important contribution to author theory. As I have suggested, Foucault's sense of what the phrase 'the death of the author' might mean is rather more carefully qualified than Barthes's and this is indicated by the fact that while Barthes gestures briefly towards a history of authorship, Foucault's essay involves a rather more determined engagement with the historicity of authorship. Although he argues that he is not offering a socio-cultural history of authorship, he does nevertheless indicate in a single sentence just what such an analysis might involve: we could research how an author becomes 'individualized', he suggests, and examine the status accorded him; we could locate the emergence of notions of authenticity and authorial attribution; we could try to understand the 'system of valoriza-tion' of authors, as well as the developing interest in authors' lives and the historical development of criticism that takes as its focus the author's life in relation to his work (p. 141). And it is in fact just such a social history of authorship that Foucault has initiated and with which he concerns himself in the remainder of the essay. Indeed, the influence of this brief, suggestive outline of what a social history of authorship might look like cannot be overestimated: it is precisely these matters that have dominated much of the discussion of authorship in the decades since the essay's first publication.

Foucault argues that what he calls the 'author-function' is designated by the author's name, and he contrasts the use of the author's name with other uses. The author's name, Foucault declares, is not 'just a proper name like the rest', rather it is a 'paradoxical singularity' (p. 146). A proper name always refers to an individual, whether or not that individual has certain characteristics. Pierre Dupont, in Foucault's example, is always Pierre Dupont, whether or not he has blue eyes, was born in Paris, is a doctor. By contrast, the author's name is directly attested by the attributions of the subject that it denotes. To say that Shakespeare, the author, did not write the sonnets ascribed to him, for example, would be significantly to alter 'the manner in which the author's name functions'. 'Shakespeare' *means*, in part, 'the author of the sonnets'. The difference is that an author's name has a 'classificatory function', it defines an *oeuvre* (pp. 146–7). By ascribing an *oeuvre* to a name, Foucault suggests, one ensures that it operates according to certain conventions, that it is allowed certain privileges, and that it carries with it a particular status. Moreover, Foucault argues, the author's name is curiously intransitive in the sense that it fails to 'pass from the interior of a discourse to the real and exterior individual who produced it'. Instead, Foucault argues, the author's name 'mark[s] off the edges of the text, revealing, or at least characterizing its mode of being' (p. 147).

Having established the author's name as a crucial element in defining the workings of the author-function, and having argued for a distinction between discourses that 'contain' an author-function and those that do not, Foucault goes on to argue that this 'function' has four general characteristics:

> (1) the author-function is linked to the juridical and institutional system that encompasses, determines, and articulates the universe of discourses.
>
> (p. 153)

In the first place, the author-function is allied to notions of ownership that fully emerge in the eighteenth century with the development of copyright laws (from 1710 in Britain and from 1793 in France and 1794 in Germany) as part of a more general development of the ideology of possessive individualism. But contained within this assertion is a characteristically Foucauldian turn: the author is constituted in its modern sense precisely in relation to a *transgression* of property:

> Once a system of ownership for texts came into being, once strict rules concerning author's rights, author–publisher relations, rights of reproduction, and related matters were enacted . . . the possibility of transgression attached to the act of writing took on, more and more, the form of an imperative peculiar to literature.

Having acquired the status of owner of the work, Foucault continues, the author 'compensated' for his new role by 'systematically practicing transgression and thereby restoring danger to a writing which was now guaranteed the benefits of ownership' (pp. 148–9). As we shall see, in Chapter 2, below, the point has been vigorously pursued, revised and indeed contested by historians of literature and of book culture and the law of copyright in the decades since the publication of Foucault's essay.

> (2) [The author-function] does not affect all discourses in the same way at all times and in all types of civilization.
>
> (p. 153)

Rather than affecting all discourses in a 'universal and constant way', the author-function is historically, culturally, economically, institutionally specific (p. 149). There is, Foucault explains, a crucial distinction between the modern, post-sixteenth-century sense of the author and the idea of the author in pre-modern or in medieval times. In the Middle Ages, he argues in a sweeping generalization, poems and other literary works tended to be 'published' anonymously. By contrast, scientific texts required the signature of the author as the guarantee of their reliability. But this 'scientific' author is not constituted in terms of individuality and subjectivity: '"Hippocrates said", "Pliny recounts", were not really formulas of an argument based on authority; they were the markers inserted in discourses that were supposed to be received as statements of demonstrated truth' (p. 149). The medieval *auctor* is precisely an authority and *as such* precisely *lacks* individuality (for more on the medieval notion of the *auctor*, see Chapter 2, below). The *auctor*-author simply speaks the truth. Foucault argues that this assumption of authorship was reversed during the seventeenth and eighteenth centuries. In a highly contentious claim, Foucault argues that at that time the author-function 'faded' in scientific discourses, which were now ascribed to a certain anonymity. In an equally contentious assertion, he comments that, by contrast, literary texts began at this time to require the insignia of the author, the author-ship of the literary text becoming precisely an aspect of its literariness (on this claim, see for example Griffin 1999). 'We now ask of each poetic or fictional text: from where does it come, who wrote it, when, under what circumstances, or beginning with what design?' (Foucault 1979: 149). Anonymity in the case of literary texts becomes, Foucault suggests, intolerable, and acceptable only as an 'enigma', a riddle to be solved (p. 150).

> (3) [The author-function] is not defined by the spontaneous attribution of a discourse to its producer, but rather by a series of specific and complex operations.
>
> (p. 153)

The author, Foucault suggests, is not the *source* of the text but simply one of the ways in which it signifies. Rather than developing 'spontaneously' as the 'attribution of a discourse to an individual', the author is 'constructed' in relation to the text's position within a particular culture (p. 150). And this construction of authorship responds to varying historical and cultural determinations: 'We do not construct a "philosophical author" as we do a "poet", just as, in the eighteenth century, one did not construct a novelist as we do today', Foucault comments (p. 150). For 'modern' literary criticism, for example, the work is explained by reference to the author: the author is a 'principle of a certain unity of writing' that 'neutralize[s] the contradictions that may emerge in a series of texts' by acting as the origin of these contradictions (p. 151). In other words, the tensions or self-contradictions within a text might be explained from, say, a Marxist perspective in terms of the subject's contradictory class status, or from a Freudian perspective in terms of his or her unacknowledged desires, his or her unconscious, or from a 'humanist' perspective in terms of a certain psychology and the ongoing vicissitudes of and variabilities in a writer's life. In each case, Foucault proposes, the particular and socio-historically specific conception of the author allows the work a unity which encompasses and ultimately explains its contradictions.

> (4) [The author-function] does not refer purely and simply to a real individual, since it can give rise simultaneously to several selves, to several subjects – positions that can be occupied by different classes of individuals.
>
> (p. 153)

The author-function is not single, not an individual – or not *simply* such. The very references within a text to its author bear this out, Foucault suggests. Such references, he argues, have a different status in 'discourses provided with the author-function' from those which lack such a 'function'. In a passage that comes close to arguing for the integrity of the so-called 'implied author' (but without the hierarchy of roles assumed in Wayne Booth's model), Foucault suggests that there is a crucial distinction between the 'author' and the 'real writer':

> Everyone knows that, in a novel narrated in the first person, neither the first person pronoun, nor the present indicative refer exactly either to the writer or to the moment in which he writes, but rather to an alter ego whose distance from the author varies, often changing in the course of the work. It would be just as wrong to equate the author with the real writer as to equate him with the fictitious speaker; the author-function is carried out and operates in the scission itself, in this division and this distance.
>
> (p. 152)

All discourses involving an author-function, Foucault goes on, 'possess this plurality of self' (p. 152). To limit the point in a way that Foucault both suggests and resists, literary texts may be said to be constructed precisely in relation to such a 'plurality' of authorial positions or 'functions'.

Ending his essay, Foucault makes three supplementary observations. The first would seem to have little bearing on the question of literature and indeed is specifically distanced from literary discourse. Here, Foucault elaborates a distinction between the author-function with respect to an individual text, work or *oeuvre* on the one hand and the 'founders of discursivity' on the other. Such 'founders of discursivity' are authors in a special sense: they are originators of a 'theory, tradition, or discipline' (p. 153). A 'founder of discursivity' for Foucault is one that has produced the 'possibilities and the rules for the formation of other texts'. Freud and Marx, to cite Foucault's examples, have not only written a number of works but have 'established an endless possibility of discourse' (p. 154). By contrast with propositions in physics or cosmology, which are affirmed 'in relation to what . . . *is*' (rather than in relation to the writings of, say,

Galileo or Newton), propositions in Marxism or psychoanalysis are judged in relation to the writings of Marx or Freud. In practising psychoanalysis or developing a Marxist analysis, one therefore continually refers back to the originator, to the 'author', of these discourses. And by contrast with physics or cosmology, any re-examination of Freud's or Marx's writings itself serves to 'modify' the discourses of psychoanalysis or Marxism (pp. 156–7). In this respect, founders of discursivity open up the paradoxical possibility not only of a development of their ideas but of the production of 'something other than their discourse, yet something belonging to what they founded' (pp. 154–5).

'What is an Author?' closes with two further remarks that have rather more immediate consequences for literary studies. In the first place, Foucault suggests that his analysis of the 'author-function', while apparently resistant to questions of subjectivity, of biography and psychology, also allows for a renewed questioning of such categories. But instead of investigating ways in which the text is determined by a governing subjectivity, by an individual's consciousness or by his or her unconscious, by the biography or the psychology of the author, such a renewed and transformed interrogation, Foucault suggests, will reverse this relation and understand subjectivity as itself part of the 'variable and complex function of discourse' itself: 'it is a matter', he comments, 'of depriving the subject (or its substitute) of its role as originator, and of analyzing the subject as a variable and complex function of discourse' (p. 158).

Finally, echoing Barthes's characterization of conventional notions of the author as 'a perpetual surging of invention' (p. 159), Foucault argues, in perhaps self-consciously melodramatic and even self-parodic terms, that his notion of the author-function can help to 'reduce the great peril, the great danger with which fiction [i.e. ideology] threatens our world' (p. 158). The author, he explains, is conventionally conceived of as a 'genial creator' who endows his work with 'infinite wealth and generosity, an inexhaustible world of signification'; he is conceived of as 'different from all other men' and as one with whom 'as soon as he speaks, meaning begins to proliferate, to proliferate indefinitely' (p. 159). In reality, Foucault declares, the author is 'a certain functional principle by which, in our culture, one limits, excludes, and chooses'. Ironically – or 'ideologically' – while we conventionally represent the author-genius as a 'perpetual surging of invention', in fact, Foucault argues that we use him or her in precisely the opposite way, to 'mark the manner in which we fear the proliferation of meaning': the author is indeed 'the principle of thrift in the proliferation of meaning' (p. 159). And yet, Foucault insists, it would be 'pure romanticism' to argue, as Barthes does, that there could be a culture in which 'the fictive would operate in an absolutely free state' without the 'necessary or constraining figure' of the author (p. 159). Foucault speculates that if the author-function disappears in the future, it will be replaced by another 'system of constraint' (p. 160). In this regard, he both argues for and warns against the idea of the disappearance or 'death' of the author. In particular, he argues against the messianic fervour of a certain teleology or end-directedness that is implied by Barthes's notion of the 'death' of the tyrannical author. As Foucault famously declares elsewhere, 'power is everywhere', even in the disappearing author (Foucault 1981: 93).

Roland Barthes and Michel Foucault laid the foundations for later literary-critical and theoretical thinking about authors. Through their overlapping, contestatory and in many ways contrasting essays, they challenge us to respond to the idea of the author's 'death' or 'disappearance' in contemporary culture and at the same time to examine more closely the historical formation of a certain conception of the relationship between text or work or oeuvre and the historical agent, the historical subject, the individual who is allegedly responsible for the production of such works, the author.

2

AUTHORITY, OWNERSHIP, ORIGINALITY

THE HISTORY OF AUTHORSHIP

Who was the first author in the Western or European tradition? Was it Homer or Hesiod (both living in *c.*700 BC, if they really existed), of whom Herodotus said that any poet who is 'supposed to have lived before [them] actually came after them' (Taplin 2000b: 9)? Was it Simonides (*c.*557/6–468 BC), said to have been the first to have accepted poetic commissions for a fee; or after him Pindar (*c.*522–443 BC) and Bakchylides (born *c.*510 BC), the 'first true authors' (Kurke 2000: 45)? Perhaps it was Virgil (70–19 BC) or Ovid (43 BC–AD 17), Dante (1265–1321) or Petrarch (1304–74), all in their different ways candidates for such a role. And who was the first English author? Was it the poet of *Beowulf* (*c.*1000), the author of the first great long poem in Old English? Was it Geoffrey Chaucer (*c.*1343–1400), with his personalized and individualized 'voice'? Or Edmund Spenser (*c.*1552–99), who rejected the constricting courtly prejudice against the 'stigma' of print to make a name for himself? Was it William Shakespeare (1564–1616), who became, after his death, the very model of the universal genius? Or Ben Jonson (*c.*1572–1637), so conscious of his literary vocation that he was one of the first to publish (in 1616) his own collected works while still alive? Was it John Milton (1608–74), who is said to have been the first writer to sign a formal contract when he sold *Paradise Lost* to Samuel Simmons for what must seem to us to be the bargain-basement price of just £5? Or Daniel Defoe (1660–1731), who earned his living through journalism and wrote two of the earliest English novels, *Robinson Crusoe* and *Moll Flanders*? Was it Alexander Pope (1688–1744), with his masterly manipulation of the newly emergent publishing industry? Or Samuel Johnson (1709–84), whose famous letter rejecting aristocratic patronage has been called the 'Magna Carta' of the modern, independent, professional writer? Or was it finally William Wordsworth (1770–1850), who had what might be thought of as a thoroughly modern obsession with self, with himself as poet, as author?

But it is an odd question, 'who was the first author?', one which is itself immersed in what we might call an authorcentric or *auteurist* ideology, in an unreflecting and perhaps rather superficial sense that literary culture is invariably based around isolated individuals, around the solitary figure of the genius. Interestingly, almost all the men, exclusively men, listed above *have* at some point been awarded the honour by critics and historians of literature. And such a list, as well as being authorcentric, illustrates something about the way in which the thinking behind such a question works. The answer to the question of who is the first author depends on which criteria one takes, whether it is sheer chronological priority or something else: individuality, print publication, transcendent and universal genius, literary self-consciousness, financial independence, or even self-obsession. The discussion is commensurate with arguments about the 'first novel', which, as Brean Hammond has observed, involve a 'retrospective process of privileging', rather than an elucidation of 'empirical fact[s]': the author, like the novel, is not 'a category intrinsic to' the object itself, but is rather a 'critical construct' of literary-historical discourse (Hammond 1997: 219). Rather than answering this peculiar question of priority, therefore, in this chapter I will discuss some of the ways in which literary history and literary theory have conceived of authors before the Romantic period, before authorship takes on its special place in what comes in that period to be institutionalized and privileged as 'Literature'. In particular, I will briefly focus on four phases in such a history: the author in ancient Greek culture; the medieval *auctor*; the influence of print on the question of authorship in the early modern period; and the importance of the invention of copyright for the establishment of the modern author in the eighteenth century.

The history of authorship is yet to be written. As far as the English tradition goes, A.S. Collins, Edwin Haviland Miller, and J.W. Saunders, all writing before Foucault, covered between them Elizabethan England (in Miller's *The Professional Writer in Elizabethan England* (1959)), the eighteenth and early nineteenth centuries (in Collins's *Authorship in the Days of Johnson* (1927) and *The Profession of Letters, 1780–1832* (1928)), and the professionalization of the writer from the medieval period to the mid-twentieth century (in Saunders's *The Profession of English Letters* (1964)). And since the early 1980s, one of the most significant developments in literary criticism has been an increasingly detailed focus on the emergence, from the Middle Ages to the Romantic period and beyond, of the modern sense of authorship, in studies which engage with the medieval period (Burrow 1982; Minnis 1988; Holmes 2000; Trigg 2002), the early modern period (Helgerson 1983; Wall 1993; Pask 1996; Masten 1997; Loewenstein 2002a; Heale 2003; North 2003), the later seventeenth and eighteenth centuries (Stewart 1991; Rose 1993; Hammond 1997; Kewes 1998), and the Romantic period itself (Leader 1996; Hofkosh 1998; Newlyn 2000; Clery *et al.* 2002), as well as with the particular conditions of female authorship from the fifteenth to the nineteenth centuries (Gilbert and Gubar 1979; Hobby 1988; Todd 1989; Turner 1992; Summit 2000). As this selective listing might suggest, the history of authorship is in the process of being written. In these and other recent studies of authorship we are beginning to see emerging a complex, albeit contested, account of that history.

THE AUTHOR IN ANCIENT GREEK CULTURE

Although Barthes's and Foucault's brief forays into the social history of authorship are based around the proposition that the 'modern' author develops out of a very different medieval dispensation, and although many historians of authorship venture no further back than the beginnings of English or French or Italian poetry, it is worth briefly attending to certain aspects of the representation of authorship in ancient Greek culture. A number of fundamental distinctions and formulations within the category of the 'modern' author can be shown to be emergent within that culture in ways that might allow us to think differently about our own conceptions of authorship.

We might start by contemplating the 'Homeric question', the centuries-old debate over the identity or identities of the poet or poets of the *Iliad* and the *Odyssey*. 'What is meant by the name *Homer*?', ask Thomas R. Walsh and Rodney Merrill in the Introduction to a recent translation of the *Odyssey*. It is a question that we 'cannot help but ask', they propose, and our answer to it will affect the 'way we experience the poem' (Walsh and Merrill 2002: 7). For Jasper Griffin, in the Introduction to another recent translation, Homer is 'simply a figure of speech' (Griffin 2000: xv). This difficulty in thinking about the 'first' poet in the European literary tradition is a consequence not just of a lack of records but of the very status of the poet in the oral culture in which he is or they are understood to have worked. Developing the ground-breaking work of Milman Parry from the 1920s and 1930s, in his classic study of the oral contexts of Homer's compositional practice, *The Singer of Tales* (1960), Albert B. Lord speculated on Homer's mode of composition by studying the (then) surviving oral epic tradition of Yugoslavia. Lord's theory of Homeric composition proposed that conventional ways of addressing the question of Homer involved anachronistic ways of thinking about the 'author-ship' of the *Iliad* and the *Odyssey*. Lord argued instead that Homer should be seen both as an individual *and* as a certain oral tradition. While not denying that Homer may in fact have been an individual who brought the poems now known as the *Iliad* and the *Odyssey* to a level of perfection that transcends every other oral epic poem that has come down to us, Lord argued that Homer inherited not only his stories but also his compositional techniques, his themes and his very linguistic 'formulas' from a tradition stretching back many centuries. Lord suggested that every performance in the oral epic tradition constitutes a new composition, that every performance is unique, and that at the same time every performance is also embedded within the tradition. According to Lord, our familiar distinction between an individualized or authorized work and a work of collaboration is inappropriate in the context of the non-literate, oral culture in which Homer's poems were produced. Such a culture may be said to operate through a 'both/and', rather than an 'either/or', logic, a logic that resists what might seem to us to be the common-sense assump-tions behind authorship itself. In the oral tradition, the 'singer' is both a

poet, a 'maker' (the meaning of the Greek *poietes*), and a reciter, a 'rhapsode' (literally a stitcher or weaver of songs). Any oral epic poem is radically
unique in a way that is different from the singularity that we might ascribe
to a written or memorized text since the oral epic is only ever heard one
time, in its single performance. But at the same time any oral epic is also
a 'repetition' of countless earlier performances: it is a singular event but
one that can, however, be repeated by different singers across the centuries.
The singer both composes and at the same time performs the 'song' or
poem; he both repeats the song and invents it as he sings. And the singer
is both an individual and part of a tradition; his song is both *a* song and
the song. As Lord suggests, it is difficult in our literate society to think of,
to imagine, this altogether different order of things:

> Our real difficulty arises from the fact that, unlike the oral poet, we
> are not accustomed to thinking in terms of fluidity. . . . It seems to
> us necessary to construct an ideal text or to seek an original, and we
> remain dissatisfied with an ever-changing phenomenon. I believe that
> once we know the facts of oral composition we must cease trying to
> find an original of any traditional song. From one point of view each
> performance is an original. From another point of view it is impossible
> to retrace the work of generations of singers to that moment when some
> singer first sang a particular song.
>
> (Lord 1960: 100)

Indeed, if we were able to be present at the early performances of a
song, Lord argues, we would be disappointed. The song must be 'repeated'
over time and *by other singers*, it must go through a process of development,
refinement, elaboration: it must become the tradition. In a sense, therefore,
in the oral epic tradition, there is no origin, since the 'origin' just is the
multiple rehearsals of a song. In the oral tradition, Lord declares, 'the idea
of an original is illogical' and the words 'author' and 'original' either have
no meaning or have 'a meaning quite different from the one usually
assigned to them' (p. 101). Homer, Lord concludes, '*is* the tradition'
(p. 147).

Building on and developing Albert Lord's work, Gregory Nagy has
recently speculated in controversial but suggestive ways about the mechanism that produces a figure such as Homer, arguing that such a figuration

takes place through a process of recomposition and 'retrojection'. In an oral culture, each time the 'same' poem or song is recited or sung, the performance is necessarily different from any other performance. Each performer of the song is also in some sense its co-author, developing and changing the song in his or her own ways. Nagy speculates that the 'originating' poet-author (Homer in this case) is actually produced retrospectively, as a back-formation, through the performers' own differentiation of themselves from the imagined originator of the song. We might imagine the oral dissemination of a poem progressing from one performer to the next, from A to B to C, and so on, with each performance building on the last. Nagy suggests that at some point in this series, say with performer M, differentiation effectively ends, and rather than attempting to develop or elaborate the song the performer attempts to stabilize it, to preserve what now comes to seem more like a finished 'text'. At this point, performer L begins to be mythologized as the author, the originator of the poem or song, and future performers come to be seen simply as reciters (*rhapsodes*) of L's original work. In Homer's case, in fact, the *rhapsodes* have a name, the 'tribe of Homer' or *Homeridai*, poets or performers whose task it was to preserve Homer's work for posterity in their own performances. Through this process, the poet 'becomes part of a myth, and the myth-making structure will appropriate his or her identity' (Nagy 1989: 38; see 35–8, and Nagy 1996a and 1996b). In principle, though, it could have been singer I or K or J that was constructed as the originating poet 'Homer'. In this respect, Nagy suggests, a poet like Homer is a back-formation, a retrojection or retrospective figuration and mythologization of individual authorship. Homer is 'retrojected as the original genius of heroic song, the proto-poet whose poetry is reproduced by a continuous succession of performers' (Nagy 1996a: 92). In other words, Homer becomes the archetypal poet (not least, for example, in his supposed blindness), through a process of what we might call *authorization*, through a process of retrospective figuration within and by the tradition. Indeed, Nagy speculates that the etymology of 'Homer' means 'he who joins together' (Nagy 1996a: 90; 1996b: 74). The name Homer in fact emerges, according to Barbara Graziosi, 'when the performer evokes the absent author' (Graziosi 2002: 48). Significantly, the task of later performers or *rhapsodes* is not only to retell the poem and to represent the speech of the characters within it, but in fact to impersonate the early poet as well (this being one of the original senses of the word *mimesis*) (Nagy 1989: 47–51). As Nagy comments, the 'rhapsode' of Homeric poems can be seen as '"acting" both the words and the persona of Homer himself' (Nagy 2003: 37).

Homeric authorship, then, is fundamentally different from that of later, literate and especially print-based cultures, cultures which rely on the possibility of a stable 'text' and, to varying degrees, on a specific relationship between text and original writer, poet or 'author'. And yet the process of the retrospective 'authorization' of the oral epic poet might also be said to share something with the authorization of writers in literate and print cultures. Cultural historians of the phenomenon of the institution of Shakespeare, to take a key example, have suggested that he comes fully into existence as the figure that is familiar to us, towering over the history of English Literature, some time in the eighteenth century. Michael Bristol, for example, declares that 'the real Shakespeare . . . doesn't actually exist at all, except as the imaginary projection of an important tradition of social desire' (Bristol 1999: 490). If authors don't exist, in other words, we have to invent them. And this, perhaps, is what happens, not only with Shakespeare but with all the other writers whose *oeuvres* involve strong projections of 'social desire': in ways that may not be entirely different from the case of 'Homer', we make them in the image of our desire for a transcendent originary unity. So the 'authorship' of Homer is precisely not the kind of authorship with which we are familiar, and yet an understanding of this hypothesis of the construction of 'Homer' in literary history might help us to understand something about our construction of more recent author-figures.

Lord argues that a traditional oral epic singer like Homer should not be seen as an artist but rather as a seer, serving religion in its widest 'and most basic' sense (Lord 1960: 220). This distinction is fundamental both to Greek and to later literary culture, and it is also one that separates earlier cultures from our own while never ceasing to be an important part of the cultural construction of authorship. While the ancient Greeks tended to distinguish poetry from prophecy, to distinguish *aoidos*, 'singer', from *mantis*, 'seer', in Hesiod at least the two are combined, and there is evidence that the two roles were originally conceived as undifferentiated. In the classical period of Greek culture (roughly the fifth to the third centuries BC), a new 'desacralized' role of *poietes* emerged, designating the professional craftsman of words, while the *aoidos* retained its connection with divine inspiration (Nagy 1989: 23–4). The history of authorship in the post-classical era can be conceived of with regard to the extent to which the poet or author is seen as divinely inspired, as sacred, as a seer, on the one hand, and as a craftsman of words whose allegiances and influence extend only to his power over language, story and rhetoric itself, on the other. The fact that it is the Roman *vatic* tradition that Sir Philip Sidney alludes to in his late sixteenth-century *An Apology for Poetry* and that Percy Bysshe Shelley recalls in his *A Defence of Poetry* in 1821, is itself a mark of just how deeply the prophetic dimension is embedded in cultural representations of the poet. But, like Thomas Gray's iconic and profoundly nostalgic image of the poet as 'Robed in the sable garb of woe, / With haggard eyes', as having a 'loose' beard and 'hoary hair' streaming 'like a meteor', and as one who 'with a master's hand and prophet's fire' strikes 'the deep sorrows of his lyre' in 'The Bard' (1755–7), such representations are deeply and indeed self-consciously anachronistic, attempting to recall and recuperate an ancient tradition of poetic narration that in fact takes us back before writing to a tradition of oral epic narrative in which the epic singer is indeed represented as a prophet or seer.

Gray's bard rails against a society from which the poet-prophet is radically alienated: his ode alludes to the tradition that Edward I put Plato's desire to banish poets from his ideal republic into homicidal practice by the simple expedient of killing them. The ode offers a violent illustration of the idea that the poet as prophet or seer is also, just because of his visionary powers, an outsider. As we shall see, this conception of the poet as outside society is fundamental to the emergence of the 'Romantic' author during the eighteenth century. But it is in fact a conception of the poet which has strong roots in ancient Greek culture. Oliver Taplin argues that ancient Greek culture establishes a 'mismatch' between creative individuals, those who are 'alienated, ahead of their times, temperamental, tortured', and society, which is seen as 'vulgar, fickle, conservative, complacent'. Taplin describes a configuration of alienated authorship that could easily stand for certain aspects of our own, of Romantic and post-Romantic, culture:

> From early days the poet was often seen as a lonely genius driven by creativity despite an unappreciative public: Euripides, and even the blind

itinerant Homer, are archetypal examples. Behind this lurks a deep-seated desire for the prophet or genius to be a marginalized, tortured figure. Some great price must be paid for superhuman talent.

(Taplin 2000a: xvii–xviii)

As we shall see, the figure of the author as uniquely separate from society is an important dimension of the construction of the Romantic author, and indeed of the modern author more generally.

As well as laying the foundations for the modern conception of literary authorship, the Greeks are usually held responsible for inventing literary theory. In view of its influence on later thinking, it is worth briefly considering what Plato has to say about poets in his *Ion* (*c*.390 BC) and *Republic* (*c*.375 BC). Plato raises two objections to poetry, both of which are based on what he calls the 'ancient quarrel between poetry and philosophy' (Plato 2001b: 79) and both of which have influential consequences for the idea of the poet. In *Ion*, Plato presents a dialogue on the nature of poetry and poetic inspiration between Socrates and one of the 'Sons of Homer', the Homeric *rhapsode* Ion. Socrates argues that the true poet works through inspiration but that this means that the poet is not 'in his right mind':

For a poet is an airy thing, winged and holy, and he is not able to make poetry until he becomes inspired and goes out of his mind and his intellect is no longer in him. As long as a human being has his intellect in his possession he will always lack the power to make poetry or sing prophecy.

(Plato 2001a: 41)

The poets themselves are 'not the ones who speak those verses', Socrates goes on: rather 'the god himself is the one who speaks, and he gives voice through them to us' (p. 42). This highly charged description of the poet as divinely inspired but as therefore ignorant and even 'out of his mind' is one that can be traced through the literary tradition to the present time. And it can work in two opposing ways, either to denigrate the poet as culturally and politically marginal, intellectually vacuous, ignorant, mad even; or it can work to celebrate the poet as standing apart from other men, as in touch with higher, non-human wisdom, as divinely mad and as outside of society but therefore better able to judge it.

In Plato's *Republic* Book X, we are presented with a different argument against the poets. Here the philosopher argues that poets should be excluded from his ideal republic because they lie. Representational poetry is unacceptable, Plato says, because it 'deforms' the minds of its audience (Plato 2001b: 67). Since an actual bed, to give the famous example, is only a representation of the idea of a bed, its 'type' or 'form', and since a picture or poem about a bed is a representation of that representation, a poet is 'two steps removed from truth' (p. 75). The poet, Plato concludes, 'establishes a bad system of government in people's minds by gratifying their irrational side . . . by creating images, and by being far removed from truth'. Poetry, he declares, has a 'terrifying capacity for deforming even good people' (p. 78). Just as Plato's *Ion* conceives of poets or *rhapsodes* as inspired, as out of their minds, so this expulsion from the ideal republic has also had a crucial if controversial influence on notions of authorship in the subsequent European literary tradition, in particular in relation to questions of the author's responsibility or irresponsibility, his morality or immorality, his ability or otherwise to reveal truth, the seriousness or frivolity of his chosen medium, and his position in relation to the social and the political.

THE MEDIEVAL *AUCTOR*

Recent critical and theoretical discussions of authorship tend to accept the assertions of both Barthes and Foucault with respect to the general claim that authorship was fundamentally different in the medieval period. Our own, modern 'categories and models for authorship', declare the editors of a recent anthology of Middle English literary theory, 'do not often overlap with what can be deduced from Middle English terminology and practice' (Wogan-Browne *et al.* 1999: 4). Medievalists often draw attention to a striking commentary on the 'making' of books by the thirteenth-century Franciscan monk St Bonaventure to illustrate the point. Bonaventure lists four ways of 'making a book', each related to a different way of conceiving its maker. The first is the *scriptor* or scribe, the copyist who 'add[s] nothing and change[s] nothing'; the second is a *compilator* or compiler, who 'put[s] together passages' from other texts which are 'not his own'; the third is a commentator, who adds his own words or commentary to those of others; the last is the *auctor*, who 'writes both his own words and others', but with his own in prime place and others' added only for purposes of confirmation' (Burrow 1982: 29–30). Bonaventure gives no particular privilege to the last category, that which may seem to be nearest to our own sense of authorship and, as J.A. Burrow comments, this sense of the writer, the writer as *auctor*, is still thought of as a person who writes the words of others as well as his own. In this sense, the medieval *auctor* is not seen as essentially separate from the scribe. Rather, he is configured as part of a continuum that extends from the 'simple' process of copying at one end to the act of 'original' composition at the other. While the two functions may seem fundamentally different to us, for Bonaventure there is no clear break between one and the other.

And yet, in another sense the medieval author, the *auctor*, the *auctor* as one of the 'authoritative Latin writers' (Minnis 1988: 1), seems to have a highly specialized, highly privileged identity, allied as it is to the question of authority and ultimately to God's authority itself. In the medieval period, Burrow explains, authority 'belongs to the *auctor*'. The title of *auctor* therefore carries with it a quite specific honour, status or prestige, and it is seen as importantly *augmenting* 'the knowledge and wisdom of humanity'. But this is also a very specialized sense of authorship and one which cannot properly be ascribed to contemporary, to vernacular twelfth-, thirteenth- and fourteenth-century writers, not least because 'the great *auctores* of the past, Christian and pagan, have already said almost everything there is to say' (Burrow 1982: 32). In *Medieval Theory of Authorship* (1984), A.J. Minnis elaborates this sense of the *auctor*. The '*auctor*', Minnis explains, was conceived as 'a writer and an authority' who ultimately takes his authority from God: he is 'someone not merely to be read but also to be respected and believed'. The *auctor* was seen as producing or possessing '*auctoritas*', authority, and as making authoritative statements, statements that could be quoted or extracted, that had credibility, that were to be believed:

> According to medieval grammarians, the term derived its meaning from four main sources: *auctor* was supposed to be related to the Latin verbs *agere* 'to act or perform', *augere* 'to grow' and *auieo* 'to tie', and to the Greek noun *autentim* 'authority'. An *auctor* 'performed' the act of writing.

He brought something into being, caused it to 'grow'. In the more specialised sense related to *auieo*, poets like Virgil and Lucan were *auctores* in that they 'tied' together their verses with feet and metres. To the ideas of achievement and growth was easily assimilated the idea of authenticity or 'authoritativeness'.

(Minnis 1988: 10)

As Donald Pease comments, such *auctores* were understood to have 'established the founding rules and principles' for the various disciplines of knowledge and to have 'sanctioned the moral and political authority of medieval culture more generally'. Thus in the medieval period, the author, as *auctor*, 'did not entail verbal inventiveness', as does his modern or romantic counterpart, but precisely its opposite (Pease 1990: 106, 105). As Minnis comments, this conception of the authority of the *auctor* was in fact strangely circular: 'the work of an *auctor* was a book worth reading; a book worth reading had to be the work of an *auctor*'. But the *auctor*, the author as unquestioned authority, by definition excluded vernacular writers: the contemporary vernacular writer simply couldn't 'decently be called an *auctor*' (Minnis 1988: 12). In this sense, authors really are dead, they even use the 'dead' languages of Greek and Latin, and the task of vernacular writers was to understand, to interpret and elaborate rather than to compete with, such authorities.

By contrast with the 'modern' sense of the author as a personalized individual expressing intentions and a particular subjectivity, the medieval *auctor* is seen as effectively, even if not always in practice, anonymous. The *auctor* in this respect is a function of his own 'culturally neutral pronouncements', his authority, his *auctoritas* (Trigg 2002: 77). And although the point should not be overplayed, manuscript culture was in practice largely anonymous with regard to vernacular writers of the early-medieval period (see Burrow 1982: 40–6). Since manually copied books were, in the first place, distributed amongst the limited circle of the writer's community, adding the writer's name to a manuscript was largely redundant. As the copied manuscript was disseminated more widely, the writer's name became irrelevant in a different, opposite sense: precisely because the writer was not known to readers outside his community, his name had little import. The contemporary vernacular writer was not after all seen as an authority but simply as one who transmits a story or some information: this wider readership was not interested in the writer, who is unknown and has little more significance to the reader than a scribe, but in the work itself and the truths that it revealed (Saunders 1964: 19–20). The manuscript, comments Peter Beal, 'eschews announcing itself', by contrast with the printed book, which 'needs, in a sense, publicly to create its own context, its own social justification, its own clientele, by displaying itself in every particular', including, on its title-page, printer, bookseller and author (Beal 1998: 18).

The medieval sense of authorship, then, involves fundamental differences from the modern sense of authors as individuals, as expressing subjective truths, as having particular 'styles' or 'voices' – even as having names. And yet even as they describe these differences, medievalists have been concerned to trace the beginnings of the emergence of the modern conception or figuration of authorship. Burt Kimmelman has recently summed up what might seem to be a paradox of medieval notions of authorship: poets of the later Middle Ages 'did indeed desire to assert themselves as poets – that is, as *auctores* – yet their enterprise took the form of an evolved sense of eloquence that in part derived from, and could be tested by, a reader's or listener's commitment to a literary past' (Kimmelman 1999: 21). In other words, one's identification as an author involved both self-assertion and a submission to the tradition. Tracing the development of the author into the late fourteenth century, Minnis argues that the medieval notion of the *auctor* as an 'authority, someone to be believed and imitated' begins to develop into an individual whose 'human qualities' began more clearly to be emphasized (Minnis 1988: 5). Indeed, as Burrow comments, the late fourteenth-century writers Chaucer, Langland and Gower 'are poets with names and identities who speak in distinctive voices' and therefore constitute the 'first generation of English writers who form a group of recognizable people' (Burrow 1982: 40, 44). And as Kimmelman comments, by the later Middle Ages, writers or authors 'creat[ed] opportunities for self-advancement, for recognition as individuals, through the very craft of authorship', not least by naming themselves and presenting themselves *as poets* within their texts (Kimmelman 1999: 7).

Despite his modest description of his role towards the end of the Prologue to *The Canterbury Tales* as one who has simply 'compiled' the text, Chaucer clearly expresses an emergent authorial self. His authorial persona and the development of that persona from poem to poem is, according to Kimmelman, Chaucer's 'major literary innovation' (Kimmelman 1999: 169). For Minnis, Chaucer's playful and self-reflexive questioning of the extent of his own responsibility for the tales that he 'rehearses' in the General Prologue to *The Canterbury Tales* articulates the beginnings of a 'modern' sense of the author as a personality, as an individual. Towards the end of the Prologue, Chaucer urges his readers not to ascribe to him the 'vileynye' of retelling the 'wordes' and 'cheere' of his characters, 'Ne thogh I speke hir wordes proprely'. For you know as well as I do, Chaucer argues, that 'Whoso shal telle a tale after a man, / He moot *reherce* as ny as evere he kan / Everich a word' however 'rudeliche and large' he might therefore be forced to 'speke' – 'Or ellis', Chaucer continues, 'he moot telle his tale untrewe, / Or feyne thyng, or fynde wordes newe' (lines 726–42; quoted in Minnis 1988: 199). In this essentially inaccurate and arguably self-protective assertion of what he wants us to believe is his own modest contribution to *The Canterbury Tales*, Chaucer depends on his reader's understanding of a tradition of writing in which the writer is presented simply as a compiler of the authorities that he cites and explicates, extending such fidelity from the *auctoritas* of the ancient authors to the rather more questionable authority of his characters (Minnis 1988: 203). In this respect, Chaucer's adoption of the role of compiler is in fact a knowing 'disguise' for his own presence as a self-conscious author. Indeed, we might go further than this and suggest that it is the very modesty by which he explains his humble position as 'compilatio' that is itself an *assertion* of authorship. He is an author, in other words, an author in the modern sense, just to the extent that he disclaims authority, to the extent that he disavows authorship, *auctoritas*: it is this knowing fiction of authorial modesty that allows us to recognize the elaborate authorial game that is set in motion in *The Canterbury Tales*. To put it simply, a large part of our enjoyment of *The Canterbury Tales*, a major aspect of the modern pleasure we take in Chaucer's poem, is our ability to perceive a gap between the characters and the author, a gap that allows us to construct, in the irony, allusions, digressive formulations, asides, textual figures, and in the exploitation and deformation of a host of literary conventions, a sense of an author.

In a recent study of the institution of Chaucer's authorship in the centuries after his death, Stephanie Trigg concurs with Minnis and Burrow in suggesting that Chaucer stands at the beginning of the development of a 'modern' conception of authorship. Chaucer, Trigg suggests, is an 'exemplary embodiment of the transitions and contradictions involved in late medieval understandings of authorship' (Trigg 2002: 54–5), and she provides a useful summary of three competing models of authorship available to Chaucer:

> First, in decline as Chaucer starts to write in English, the socially oriented role of the *poet* performing before a group; second, the more individually oriented role of the *writer* working with the inherited textual tradition, the dominant mode of late medieval textuality; and third, Chaucer's anticipation of an emerging, modern understanding of the professional *author* setting the terms for his own posterity.
>
> (Trigg 2002: 50)

Trigg argues that what is distinctive about Chaucer's works is that they invite 'sympathetic readerly identifications' with the narrator-figure, who acts as a kind of stand-in for the author, and she proposes that such identifications are themselves intrinsic to post-Romantic understandings of literary texts (Trigg 2002: xviii). But as Trigg suggests, it is the later *reception* of Chaucer that truly embeds him within a modern understanding of authorship. The idea that Chaucer constitutes the 'intentional, sentient genesis of the work' allows for intentionalist or biographical readings. But it is also fundamental to discussions of Chaucer's irony, omniscience, and narrative voice and is ultimately behind the whole institution of Chaucer studies. But this is an anachronistic conception of Chaucer, Trigg suggests, an imposition of later conceptions of authorship back onto the fourteenth-century poet. The point is made clear in a telling comment by J.A. Burrow: 'in those works which still interest us', he affirms, the conventional assertion of an author's dependence upon prior texts 'proves to be partially illusory' (Burrow 1982: 34). In other words, it is precisely those works that can be conceived of as proposing a 'modern', even 'Romantic' sense of the author as originator, as *not* finally dependent on the tradition, that have survived, that have entered the canon, that live on in a literary tradition that increasingly requires just such signs of authorial individuality for its interest to be provoked.

PRINT CULTURE

The dissemination of written works in a manuscript culture entails the repeated manual copying of texts. Unlike a printed text, over which the writer can, in principle at least, have almost complete control, the 'publication' of a manuscript, with its multiple copying by successive scribes severely limits the writer's ability to stabilize the text. And in fact in a manuscript culture the scribe's name is as likely to appear on a text as that of the author, the author often being 'lost in anonymity' (Saunders 1964: 18). As Arthur Marotti comments:

> In the system of manuscript transmission, it was normal for lyrics to elicit revisions, corrections, supplements, and answers, for they were part of an ongoing social discourse. In this environment texts were inherently malleable, escaping authorial control to enter a social world in which recipients both consciously and unconsciously altered what they received.
>
> (Marotti 1995: 135)

The system was, Marotti concludes, 'far less author centred' than was print culture.

One of the consequences of the invention of movable type in the late fifteenth century was the potential regularization of the published work. While some critics have argued that writing, that literate culture, is the necessary precondition for the establishment or invention of the modern sense of authorship, in her study of the development of print culture in early modern Europe, *The Printing Press as an Agent of Change* (1979), Elizabeth Eisenstein argues that, from its introduction, the new technology of print publication was closely connected to new conceptions of authorship. Eisenstein comments that while the 'urge to scribble' was no doubt as common in ancient Rome as it was in, say, Renaissance Florence, there is an important difference between seeing one's work and one's name in a fixed, permanent form on the one hand and writing verses that might be 'lost forever, altered by copying, or – if truly memorable – be carried by oral transmission and assigned ultimately to "anon"' on the other. 'Until it became possible to distinguish between composing a poem and reciting one, or writing a book and copying one', and until books could be classified by their authors' names, Eisenstein asks, 'how could modern games of books and authors be played?' (1979: 1.121). Similarly, she argues that originality, the crux of, the determining element in, modern conceptions of authorship, has an entirely different status in the 'age of scribes' since without the disseminatory potential for relatively cheap, relatively speedy multiple copies that print affords, no one would have been in a position to know that a new discovery was in fact new (1.123–4). For this reason, Burrow distinguishes between the '"intermittent" culture of the manuscript age and the "continuous, incremental" culture of the age of print' (Burrow 1982: 126). Before the establishment of a print culture, Eisenstein suggests, writing was thought of in terms of the representation of what is already known. In such a culture, invention is what, in a different context, Jacques Derrida calls '*revelatory* invention, the discovering and unveiling of what *already* is' as opposed to the production of something new, what he calls 'creative invention, the production of what is not' (Derrida 2002: 168).

Eisenstein links the new emphasis on the individual in the Renaissance to print culture: printing, she suggests, leads to the need for new kinds of property rights that come to be known as 'copyright', and such rights ultimately lead to an increase in prestige for inventors or authors (Eisenstein 1979: 1.240). But printing also leads to a counter-reaction, against the uniformity and standardization that it necessitates, and, as Wendy Wall has commented in her study of *The Imprint of Gender: Authorship and Publication in the English Renaissance* (1993), authorship in the early modern period may be seen as having been redefined in the context of the 'print industry's *collision* with manuscript culture' (Wall 1993: xi; italics added). Just as the later Romantic emphasis on the subjectivity of an isolated individual involved a reaction against the alleged dehumanizing qualities of industrialization, so the uniformity of the printed book (itself, of course, an important agent in the process of industrialization) led to a desire to express one's personality, one's self, to represent oneself as a unique individual, and to gain what Walter Benjamin might call the 'aura' of individuality (Eisenstein 1979: 230–5; see Benjamin 2001: 1169). For some historians, then, print culture leads to a renewed emphasis on individuality precisely in reaction *against* its uniformalizing impulse. By contrast, others have discerned within the new culture of the printed book itself opportunities for the expression of a new individuality. Walter Ong, for example, argues that the formal properties of the printed book offer the illusion of a thing apart, and suggests that while oral culture assumes intertextuality, with one poem or story building on another, the printed book in particular gives the illusion of being quite separate from other texts, producing a strong effect of 'closure' which also in turn affirms the individuality, originality and separateness of the author (Ong 1982: 133–4). Whether print culture is understood to produce a threatening uniformity and an assertion of individuality as a reaction, or to confirm individuality in its formal qualities of closure and distinction, it undoubtedly entails a new relationship between text and author. This new, commercial relationship is expressed in a strengthening of the sense of the individuality and privacy of acts of reading and writing, and in the eventual development of legally constituted rights of authorial ownership (see North 2001: 1380). By the mid-sixteenth century, Elizabeth Heale remarks, 'kinds of writing in which the subject could be figured as both authorial and self-expressive, however tentative and unstable its fictions, had become a commonly acknowledged discursive possibility' (Heale 2003: 5).

In the transitional period of the sixteenth century, the formation of the emerging and developing category of the literary author seems to have been located in what Wendy Wall characterizes as the 'collision between manuscript and print practices on the one hand, and between aristocratic amateurism and the marketplace on the other' (Wall 1993: 3). Well into the seventeenth century, in fact, the relationship between poetry and print publication was highly unstable, with print publication commonly seen as degrading to the art of poetry: 'the relentless democratization of literature', as Beal puts it, results in 'an ever-increasing sense of its degeneracy' (Beal 1998: 30). The development of a market for printed books, at least so far as imaginative works were concerned, was inhibited by an aristocratic, courtly disdain for the professionalization of writing, and a prejudice against publication in print on account of its perceived propensity to undermine the fragile class boundary between the aristocracy and the lower gentry. 'Because gentlemanly amateurism was a vital part of court culture', comments Wall of the second half of the sixteenth century, writers 'found it expedient to endorse the idea that publication made one common and vulgar' (Wall 1993: x). As Saunders comments, court writers 'never threw off' the fiction of 'a quasi-medieval humility about their own works' (Saunders 1964: 47). The courtier gained his prestige and his wealth from his position in court and the attempt to earn either wealth or position from publication was seen as both an unnecessary and a disreputable degradation of one's aristocratic status, or of one's aspirations to such status. 'What greater and more odious infamye, for on[e] of my standinge in the Universitye and profession abroade', writes Gabriel Harvey to Edmund Spenser towards the end of the sixteenth century, than to be classed amongst 'Inglish Rimers?' (quoted in Saunders 1964: 49). In her study of the importance of print for the institution and masculinization of authorship, Wall sums up the cultural tensions between print and manuscript circulation as follows:

> Renaissance manuscripts were collectively produced and permeable texts, subject to editorial revision as they were passed from hand to hand. These works derived authority from their place in coterie circles – at court and in the satellite environments of the Inns of Court and the universities. Printed texts, on the other hand, can be said to have been authorized by an appeal to their intrinsic textual features rather than to their status as occasional verse. Because they were linked to merchandising, however, printed texts had considerably less social authority.
>
> (Wall 1993: 8)

Saunders comments that while writers might receive payment of some kind for their work, the work itself was not 'the immediate *raison d'être* of the system' (Saunders 1964: 43). Rather, poetic composition was seen as a way of gaining favour with a rich and powerful patron by a display of wit and intellectual ingenuity, an ability that might then be translated into some other employment more directly useful to the patron (Helgerson 1983: 29). Writers were able, through verse, to 'display themselves to potential patrons, as courtly, verbally adept, morally reliable, men well equipped for employment as secretaries, clerks in official service, private tutors, or as witty producers of aristocratic entertainments' (Heale 2003: 11). Indeed, Wendy Wall goes so far as to declare that Renaissance writers 'could not easily identify themselves as "authors" in the modern or ancient sense of the term' because of 'the prestige attached to poetic amateurism, the vitality of the institution of patronage, [and] the court's curbs on channels of ambition' (Wall 1993: 12–13). In other words, historians have located the modern sense of authorship as firmly wedded to questions not only of technology but also of economics. So long as it is not economically viable for an individual to make his or her living from writing, rather than from patronage, a modern sense of authorship remains dormant or only partly articulated within the dominant culture. It is only with a reduction in the prestige, status and financial and political power of the court, a reduction that goes along with the growth of the mercantile classes and the increasing financial opportunities made available by print technology, that the profession of authorship, that authorship as a profession, can emerge.

It is in fact precisely those poets of the sixteenth and seventeenth centuries that challenged the 'stigma' of print, who embraced, in their own ways, authorship as a profession, that may be said to have succeeded in positioning themselves at the centre of the English literary canon. There seems to be something of an uncanny literary-historical logic in such canonization, one that was to be developed and embraced into a fully-fledged 'culture of posterity' in the eighteenth century and the Romantic period (see Bennett 1999 and 2005a): poets are memorialized in the future just to the extent that they escape the prejudices of their own time and embrace what will become the standards of posterity. Richard Helgerson examines the emergence of this logic of canonization in a study of the literary 'system' out of which Spenser, Jonson and Milton emerged, *Self-Crowned Laureates* (1983). Helgerson distinguishes between the courtly 'amateurs' of the sixteenth and early seventeenth centuries and those 'professionals' that he calls 'laureate poets'. 'Laureate' poets are those whose writing was itself 'a means of making a contribution to the order and improvement of the state' (Helgerson 1983: 29), poets whose ambition resided in poetry alone and who embraced print technology and the potential fame and wealth it could bring. As seems to have been the case with Chaucer, Helgerson's three laureate poets, Spenser, Jonson and Milton, were all concerned with their own status and role as poets, with themselves as authors. Spenser, Helgerson comments, was 'unique' amongst his contemporaries, since he alone 'presented himself as a poet, as a man who considered writing a duty rather than a distraction', and was England's first 'professed, if not fully professional, poet' (pp. 55, 82). Jonson's 'work was himself', Helgerson comments, 'and he could not avoid saying so': 'No other English Renaissance poet so intrudes on his work', and he insists on 'his laureate self-presentation' to such an extent that 'sometimes the poet overwhelms the poem' (pp. 182, 183, 103). And Milton 'transcend[s] the difficulties inherent in his temporal location', his 'grandly imposing solitariness' itself figuring amongst 'the most persistent and most powerful signs of [his] laureate transcendence' (pp. 231, 235). If Helgerson is right, the origin of the modern or Romantic sense of authorship in the English canon involves a self-conscious insistence on the poet him- or herself as poet, an idea that confirms Lawrence Lipking's more general, and more historically unspecific, idea that poets become poets precisely by meditating on what it means to be a poet: 'Every major Western poet after Homer', comments Lipking, 'has left some work that records the principles of his own poetic development' (Lipking 1981: viii). What ultimately marks out Helgerson's 'laureate' poets is precisely that they embrace print culture and thereby self-consciously mark themselves out, that they therefore constitute individual voices and personalities, that they make themselves into authors in a sense that can only be fully appreciated after their death.

THE INVENTION OF COPYRIGHT

Literary historians tend to agree that the crucial social and commercial changes that brought about the invention of the modern sense of authorship occurred in the seventeenth and eighteenth centuries, once print technology had become firmly embedded within the culture of Western Europe and once its 'stigma' had been ameliorated by its financial rewards – by the possibility, at least, that one can make a living by writing. Brean Hammond usefully sums up the commercial and cultural pressures occurring in the wake of and partly as a result of the English civil war in the mid-seventeenth century as Britain is transformed into a mass consumer society and as poetry and other literary works become a significant part of what Pierre Bourdieu calls 'cultural capital':

> Demand for printed materials is recognized to have been stimulated by the Civil War itself, and literacy rates, steadily rising throughout the early modern period, are thought to have grown especially fast, and particularly amongst women, in the decades following the Restoration.

In a society becoming capable of delivering a standard of living considerably above that of mere subsistence to an increasing number of its members, books were amongst the possessions that these improving citizens wanted to consume. Indeed, they were high on the list of such consumables, because, as people grew richer, they required the trappings of what David Hume would call 'refinement' to distance themselves from those who could not afford to acquire it and to narrow the gap between themselves and those who had possessed such refinement effortlessly for several generations. By the 1690s, when newspapers and periodicals . . . had become a permanent part of the publishing scene, we can speak of the beginnings of a mass market for literature. Publishers were trying to locate it with ever-greater precision and directness, writers were responding to their sense of what comprised it and trying to stimulate it, and readers were eager to participate in it. Writing could not remain what it had been – manuscript material circulated narrowly amongst coteries or inaccessible printed books, the production of which was supported by noble patrons.

(Hammond 1997: 32)

These are the conditions in which the author in the modern sense emerges, the author, that is to say, as an individual dedicated to writing and dependent on writing either for a living or for a sense of identity, the author as autonomous and as independent of patronage and ultimately of society itself. And historians tend to agree that the emergence of this sense of authorship is a function of, and reflected in, changes to the legal status of published writers, changes which are in turn a consequence of the burgeoning culture of print.

In his study of the relationship between authorship and the law of copyright, *Authors and Owners: The Invention of Copyright* (1993), Mark Rose argues that the invention of authorship in the modern sense is 'inseparable from the commodification of literature', and that the 'distinguishing characteristic' of the modern author is 'proprietorship': the 'invention' of British copyright in 1710 affirms the new conception of the author as the 'originator and therefore the owner of a special kind of commodity, the work' (Rose 1993: 1–2). Rose suggests that there is a transformation in the conception of authorship from a sixteenth- and early seventeenth-century emphasis on what the poet *does* towards a clearer sense of the author as owning a certain property – 'intellectual property', as it eventually comes to be known – associated with the growth in possessive individualism in the later seventeenth-century (pp. 13–15). Martha Woodmansee goes further when she allies the modern notion of authorship with the legal concept of proprietary authorship figured in the Romantic idealization of the solitary author: 'Our laws of intellectual property', she argues, 'are rooted in the century-long reconceptualization of the creative process which culminated in high Romantic pronouncements like Wordsworth's to the effect that this process *ought* to be solitary, or individual, and introduce "a new element into the intellectual universe"' (Woodmansee 1994b: 27).

The context for such arguments is the lapse of the 1662 Licensing Act in 1695. Before 1695, the publication of books was organized through the Stationers' Company, representing a limited number of London booksellers, who held a monopoly over the printing and distribution of books. After its lapse in 1695, there was a pressing need to enforce the rights, as they saw them, of booksellers over the books that they printed and sold. In 1710, an act designed to protect these rights finally came before parliament. The title of the act is itself instructive: 'An Act for the encouragement of Learning by vesting the copies of printed books in the authors or purchasers of such copies during the times therein mentioned'. In other words, the act is directed towards the 'advancement of Learning', rather than towards the advancement of the rights of authors. As John Feather comments, the 'driving force' behind the recognition of authors' rights was economic: copyright was a 'device developed . . . to protect the investments of those involved in printing and publishing' rather than having to do with more 'elevated' matters of purely literary interest (Feather 1994: 4–5). Indeed, authors and booksellers or publishers are treated as equivalent: copyright belongs either to the author or to those to whom the author sells his or her 'copy'. Nevertheless, as an unintended consequence of the need to protect publishers' rights, the law instituted the author as a legal entity (Rose 1993: 49). Far from ending debate over the ownership of literary works, though, the so-called 'Statute of Anne' of 1710 prepared the way for more than a century of struggle over the precise nature of copyright, of the ownership of literary and other texts, and of the role of authors, printers and booksellers. As Rose and others have argued, the question of the legal status of literary property in the eighteenth century can be seen not only as a legal and commercial question, of the ownership of the work, but also as a contest over the very conception of authorship itself. And what the 1710 and subsequent acts of parliament finally allowed for was that the ownership of a work lies with the author (who is at liberty to sell that right on to a printer or bookseller). In other words, it was the 1710 act and its later revisions and modifications that allowed the author gradually to come into legal existence.

It is at this point that the central, the *commercial* paradox of modern or Romantic authorship begins fully to be expressed. Just at the time that authorship becomes financially and legally viable, an 'aesthetic ideology' of the transcendent and autonomous artistic work and of the author as guarantor of the originality and autonomy of that work comes into play. What has been called the 'Romantic ideology' of authorship is, in Pierre Bourdieu's phrase, an 'economic world reversed', a world in which the *value* of a work is precisely equated with its supposed distance from its 'field of production' (Bourdieu 1993: ch. 1). To put it briefly, if a book has commercial value it is seen to lack aesthetic value. The illusion is expressed by Alexander Pope, 'a consummate professional writer', as Hammond puts it, 'whose major poems stand as an attack on professional and commercial writing': 'I writ because it amused me', Pope declares, 'I corrected because it was as pleasant to me to correct as to write; and I publish'd because I was told I might please such as it was a credit to please' (Hammond 1997: 292–4).

The idea of the valueless value of the literary work, of the work as aesthetically valuable because financially worthless, is by no means new in the eighteenth century. It can, in fact, be traced back at least as far as Pindar writing in the fifth century BC and castigating the 'mercenary Muse' precisely because he himself had benefited financially from writing (see Nagy 1989: 20–1). And it is part of what we have seen was a powerful prejudice surrounding the 'stigma of print' in the sixteenth century. But it is in the eighteenth century that this ideology of authorship comes to dominate the institution of literature and begins to define a certain conception of authorship itself. As Terry Eagleton somewhat cynically comments, this representation of art and therefore of the artist as autonomous and disinterested, produced 'just when the artist is becoming debased to a petty commodity producer', may be understood to involve something of a 'spiritual compensation' for the humiliation that such an individual might feel at the prospect of writing for money (Eagleton 1990: 64–5). The paradox is that it is precisely this mystificatory sense of the author as above and beyond commercial considerations that makes his work economically or commercially viable. As Bourdieu points out in his analysis of the French nineteenth-century novelist Gustave Flaubert, the author pits himself against the 'bourgeois', sacrifices himself, 'invents himself *in suffering*, in revolt against the bourgeois, against money, by inventing a separate world where the laws of economic necessity are suspended, at least for a while, and where value is not measured by commercial success' (Bourdieu 1993: 169). This 'cultural capital' is based on a disavowal of capital, of capitalism, of the economic or mercenary motivation for writing: that, that disavowal of money, is, in the long run, what makes the money.

In this context, Roger Chartier has proposed a modification of Foucault's idea that a 'radical reversal' occurred in the seventeenth and eighteenth centuries when the 'rules for the attribution of texts belonging to "scientific" and "literary" discourse were exchanged' (Chartier 1994: 31). Instead, Chartier argues, we should focus more closely on the change from a patronage system to a commercial system of publication in the second half of the eighteenth century:

> Before, the author's subjection to obligations created by client relations and patronage ties was accompanied by a radical incommensurability between literary works and economic transactions. After the mid-century the situation was reversed when a possible and necessary monetary appreciation of literary compositions, remunerated as labour and subject to the laws of the market, was founded on an ideology of creative and disinterested genius that guaranteed the originality of the work.
>
> (p. 38)

Certainly it is true that the 'author-function' in the eighteenth century prominently involved ruses that might be seen, from one perspective, as the last gasps of a dying culture: anonymous and pseudonymous publication, the creation of 'apocryphal' or forged authors such as James Macpherson's Ossian (*Fingal* (1762), *Temora* (1763)) and Chatterton's Thomas Rowley (the 'Rowley' poems were first published in 1777), and the ascription of a (fictitious) *editorial* role for the author in novels such as Samuel Richardson's *Clarissa* (1747–9) and Henry McKenzie's *The Man of Feeling* (1771), novels which followed, in their different ways, the lead of Moll Flanders's autobiography (Daniel Defoe's *The Fortunes and Misfortunes of the Famous Moll Flanders* (1722)) and Lemuel Gulliver's travel book (Jonathan Swift's *Gulliver's Travels* (1726)). From another perspective, though, such anonymizing and pseudonymizing gestures may in fact be seen as concentrating attention on authors, on authorialism, precisely by provoking an interest in the true originator of the text. They may indeed be said to express what Susan Stewart calls a 'crisis in authenticity' (Stewart 1991: 5). Either way, the new authorial and literary regime that emerged in the eighteenth century involved a logic and economics that foregrounded authorship, increasingly insisting on the publication of the person of the author, the originator and owner of the work; and it also increasingly disavowed both an aristocratic ideology that presented the author as a gentleman scornful of print, and the mercenary, mercantile arrangements of print publication. It is this formulation of authorship that will be fully expressed in the Romantic period and that will become the conception of authorship that will be accepted and challenged over the next two centuries. In the next chapter, we will look in more detail at the idea of the Romantic author that arose out of this conception, at the author as original, autonomous, and fundamentally expressive of a unique individuality.

3

THE ROMANTIC AUTHOR

Roland Barthes and Michel Foucault, the two *authors*, in a sense, of modern author theory, both identify the late eighteenth and early nine-teenth centuries as the period in which the 'modern' conception of authorship is fully articulated. In other words, both suggest that the idea of the literary work as fundamentally, indeed exclusively, structured around the expression of an author reached its apotheosis in the period now commonly characterized by the term 'Romanticism'. As Seán Burke comments, the 'crucial historical change in conceptions of authorship' is not a function of late twentieth-century theorizing so much as of the 'romantic revolutions and the eighteenth-century philosophical and aesthetic discourses upon which it drew'. But as Burke goes on to suggest, it is precisely in Romanticism, in the tradition against which contemporary literary theory reacts with its assertion of the author's death or disap-pearance, that the metaphorical 'death' of the author is also inaugurated and theorized (Burke 1995: xix). The Romantics, in other words, both inaugurated a certain sense of authorship and, at the same time, in the very same breath, announced the author's imminent demise. Thus, the idea of the author as originator and genius, as fully intentional, fully sentient source of the literary text, as authority for and limitation on the 'proliferating' meanings of the text, has particular importance for a culture that also, at the same time, begins to extol the virtues of a 'disinterested' aesthetic, of impersonality.

In this chapter I want to examine some of the ways in which the figure of the expressive author comes to prominence in the Romantic period, a period of the most energetic theorizing about literature and literary creation. The Romantic theory of authorship, in which the author is designated as autonomous, original and expressive, may be said to account for everything that is commonly or conventionally taken to be implied by talk of 'the author' and certainly much that Barthes and Foucault take exception to in their critiques of authorship. Indeed, the debates in literary criticism and theory of the last two hundred years would have been very different without such a model of authorship. At the same time, as I have tried to suggest in Chapter 2, above, literary texts and debates in poetics and literary theory before the late eighteenth century tend to be seen through our Romantic or post-Romantic notions of authorship. Romantic theory involves what M.M. Bakhtin calls a 'crisis of authorship': Romanticism is the era in which 'the point is not to surpass others in art, but to surpass art itself' (Bakhtin 1990: 202). In this chapter, I shall attempt to indicate ways in which the Romantic, expressive theory of authorship *works*, to trace its implications and elaborations with regard to questions of composition, imagination, inspiration and originality. But I shall also explore ways in which Romantic theories of authorship are themselves open to question, themselves sites of contestation, contradiction and paradox. In other words, I want to explore ways in which the Romantic theory of authorship works precisely in and through its failure to work.

EXPRESSION, GENIUS AND ORIGINALITY

As we have seen, recent studies in the history of authorship suggest that the 'modern' configuration of authorship is related to developments in legal, political, economic, commercial, and other discourses, to the spread of and innovations in print technology, and to changes in the legal constitution of literary ownership and commercial society. Critics, historians and theorists tend to agree that these developments culminated in the second half of the eighteenth century in a redefinition of both the author and 'literature' in what comes to be known as 'Romanticism'. But the Romantic conception of authorship, with its stress on individuality, on uniqueness and originality, on the conscious intention of the autonomous subject, has also been seen as part of a more general development of the idea of the self. The very idea of the individual, upon which the modern conception of the author depends, is, Raymond Williams comments, related to the 'break-up of the medieval social, economic and religious order', with its feudalistic emphasis on a person's place in that relatively rigid hierarchy (Williams 1988: 163). Although the 'discovery of individuality' has been dated from as early as the period 1050–1200 in the English tradition (Burrow 1982: 40; Kimmelman 1999: 18–21), and although individuality is fundamental to facets of classical culture, according to Williams and others, a new individualistic order based around a particular emphasis on the subject's 'personal existence', an emphasis that can be related to Protestantism's insistence on the priority of the individual's direct and personal relationship with God, emerges in the early modern period. And Williams argues that in the late seventeenth and eighteenth centuries, logic, mathematics, and political philosophy emphasized the individual as having an 'initial and primary existence' from which 'laws and forms of society' were derived. At the same time, Williams argues, the 'individual' was also the 'starting point' for classical eighteenth-century liberalism (Williams 1988: 164). In a study of the eighteenth-century reception of William Shakespeare, Margreta De Grazia comments that this sense of individuality and self-ownership extends also to the individual subject's relationship with language itself: 'Socially, politically, and epistemologically enfranchised, the individual takes possession of language', she remarks, 'converting a discursive and transactional mode into a personalized and self-expressive one that makes language a convoluted allegory of consciousness' (De Grazia 1991: 8). John Locke's *An Essay Concerning Human Understanding* (1690) is often cited in this context. Locke argues against the 'authority' of others' opinions, and that our very knowledge of the world must itself be ours and ours alone. We should, he says, make use 'rather of our own Thoughts, than other Mens' to gain knowledge. The argument marks a major shift in the conception of knowledge, and allows for a privileging of the autonomous, individualistic author in the next century:

> For, I think, we may as rationally hope to see with other Mens Eyes, as to know by other Mens Understandings. So much as we our selves

> consider and comprehend of Truth and Reason, so much we possess
> of real and true Knowledge. The floating of other Mens Opinions in
> our brains makes us not one jot the more knowing, though they happen
> to be true. What in them was Science, is in us but Opiniatrety, whilst
> we give up our Assent to reverend Names, and do not, as they did,
> employ our own Reason to *understand* those *Truths*, which gave them
> reputation.

(Locke 1975: 101)

The eighteenth-century philosophical, commercial and political emphasis on individuality, with its ideology of possessive individualism and its special privileging of authorial autonomy, is bound up with a transformation in the value of the idea of originality. The Renaissance conception of the author gradually moved away from the medievalist sense of the author as *auctor*, as 'authority', and from the classical idea of composition as 'mimetic', as essentially involving the reproduction of generic, discursive, stylistic and formal traditions (see Vickers 1999). By the mid-eighteenth century, the notion of originality has become central to a conception of a newly empowered author. Although his book is only one statement in a more general cultural privileging of originality mid-century, the idea of literary or artistic originality is perhaps most clearly articulated in Edward Young's *Conjectures on Original Composition* (1759). Young argues that there is a fundamental distinction between 'imitators' and 'originals'. Imitators, he argues, present 'duplicates of what we have, possibly much better, before': they serve to 'increas[e] the mere drug of books' by simply 'build[ing] on another's foundation' (Young 1918: 7). Drawing no doubt on the cliché of 'apish imitation', Young points out scathingly that monkeys are 'masters of mimickry' (p. 20). Originals, he declares, in unabashedly imperialistic rhetoric, are by contrast 'great benefactors': they 'extend the republic of letters, and add a new province to its dominion' (pp. 6–7). The respective valuations that Young proposes for originality and imitation are vividly encapsulated in a passage in which he compares the genius (original) to learning (imitation):

> Learning we thank, genius we revere; That gives us pleasure, This gives
> us rapture; That informs, This inspires; and is itself inspired; for genius
> is from heaven, learning from man: *This* sets us above the low, and

illiterate; *That*, above the learned, and polite. Learning is borrowed knowledge; genius is knowledge innate, and quite our own.

(p. 17)

By aligning a certain conception of authorship with originality and therefore with 'genius', Young insists on the true author as radically independent, autonomous, and self-creating. As Françoise Meltzer puts it, 'Author, new, original, and spontaneous are the good words opposed to the bad: copyist, old, imitative (or stolen), and deliberate' (Meltzer 1994: 72). In the Romantic period in particular, this notion of originality develops into the mantra of a poet being ahead of his time, into the idea that the true poet, the genius, is original to such an extent that he will necessarily be neglected in his own time and only fully appreciated in the future, after his death. The 'original' author must, as Wordsworth puts it in an 1815 essay, 'creat[e] the taste by which he is to be enjoyed' (Wordsworth 1984: 657–8; see Bennett 1999 and 2005a).

In his classic study of the theory of romantic poetics, *The Mirror and the Lamp* (1953), M.H. Abrams argues that during the eighteenth century the dominant model of literary creation was transformed from that of a mirror held up to nature to one in which the author is like a lamp, emitting light from a singular origin or source. Abrams uses the metaphor of the lamp to describe the way that Romanticism figures poetry as 'the overflow, utterance or projection of the thoughts and feelings of the poet'. In this expressive theory of literary composition, Abrams argues, the work of literature 'ceases . . . to be regarded as primarily a reflection of nature': instead, 'the mirror held up to nature becomes transparent and yields the reader insights into the mind and heart of the poet himself' (Abrams 1953: 21–3). Influenced in part at least by what the late eighteenth-century German philosopher Immanuel Kant himself described as his 'Copernican revolution' in the theory of knowledge (epistemology), writers and philosophers in Britain and Germany in particular were concerned to place the authorial subject at the centre of the literary universe. While Lockean epistemology posited that knowledge arises out of an individual's sensation and reflection on or of the world, Kant's critical idealism proposed that our understanding of the world is contingent upon the structure of the human mind, on what Percy Bysshe Shelley calls the 'human mind's imaginings' ('Mont Blanc', 1817). The point is perhaps most memorably summed up in a parenthetical phrase from William Wordsworth's 'Tintern Abbey' (1798), where he refers to 'all that we behold / From this green earth, of all the mighty world / Of eye and ear (both what they half-create / And what perceive)' (ll. 105–8). This refiguring of eye and ear as themselves 'creative' – half-creating and half-perceiving the world – has profound implications for thinking about authors in particular.

As we have seen, this rethinking of the role of the author in the eighteenth century places an increasing emphasis on the classical idea of the author as fundamentally apart from, fundamentally separate from, society. Indeed, the Romantic author is ultimately seen as different from humanity itself. He is seen as both an exemplary human and somehow above or beyond the human, as literally and figuratively *outstanding*. He is, after all, ahead of his time, avant-garde. The idea of the Romantic author is opposed to the idea of the writer, the scribbler, the journalist or literary drudge and is conceived as a subject inspired by forces outside himself, forces that allow him to produce work of originality and genius. But this originality is itself profoundly strange. It is, at some level, inexplicable. Genius, Young argues, involves 'the power of accomplishing great things without the means generally reputed necessary to that end' (Young 1918: 13). Such a formulation points to a crucial paradox of Romantic authorship: in the ideal author, in the genius, there is a mysterious disjunction of cause and effect. There is no reason why the genius is able to create the works that he creates. This idea that the genius is both himself and beyond himself is something of a commonplace in Romantic poetics. For Kant, for example, art 'must not have the appearance of being intentional' and in fact the author 'does not himself know how the ideas' for his work 'have entered into his head' (Kant 1952: 167, 169). Similarly, Coleridge declares in an 1818 lecture on European literature that genius involves 'unconscious activity' and that this activity is itself '*the* Genius in the man of Genius' (Coleridge 1987: 2.222). Such comments are often linked to the notion of creative inspiration as well as to genius and the sublime. In his *Essay on Genius* (1774), for example, Alexander Gerard had argued that 'the fire of genius, like a divine impulse, raises the mind above itself, and by the natural influence of imagination actuates it as if it were supernaturally inspired' (Gerard 1961: 894). More prosaically, in an essay entitled, precisely, 'Whether Genius is Conscious of its Powers?' (1823), William Hazlitt declared that the very definition of genius is 'that it acts unconsciously' and that 'those who have produced immortal works, have done so without knowing how or why': Shakespeare, he declares, 'owed almost every thing to chance, scarce any thing to industry or design' (Hazlitt 1930–4: 12.118). At its most radical, William Blake declares that he has written *Milton* (1803–8) 'from immediate Dictation . . . without Premeditation & even against my Will' (Blake 1965: 697).

One of the clearest and most intriguing statements of Romanticism's belief in an 'ideal' poet comes in Coleridge's troubled and troubling literary biography, *Biographia Literaria*. As we have seen (see p. 3, above), Coleridge follows his friend Wordsworth in posing the question 'what is poetry?' Coleridge's answer is that the question is 'so nearly the same' as the question 'what is a poet?' that 'the answer to the one is involved in the solution of the other' (Coleridge 1983: 2.15). This is one of the central claims of Romanticism and one which directly links poetry, or, more generally, literature, with the author. Coleridge's explanation of the word 'poet' is instructive and is worth quoting at some length:

> For it is a distinction resulting from the poetic genius itself, which sustains and modifies the images, thoughts, and emotions of the poet's own mind. The poet, described in *ideal* perfection, brings the whole soul of man into activity, with the subordination of its faculties to each other, according to their relative worth and dignity. He diffuses a tone, and spirit of unity, that blends, and (as it were) *fuses*, each into each, by that synthetic and magical power, to which we have exclusively appropriated the name of imagination. This power, first put in action by the will and understanding, and retained under their irremissive, though gentle and unnoticed, controul . . . reveals itself in the balance or reconciliation of opposite or discordant qualities: of sameness, with difference; of the general, with the concrete; the idea, with the image; the individual, with the representative; the sense of novelty and freshness, with old and familiar objects; a more than usual state of emotion, with more than usual order; judgement ever awake and steady self-possession, with enthusiasm and feeling profound and vehement; and while it blends and harmonizes the natural and the artificial, still subordinates art to nature; the manner to the matter; and our admiration of the poet to our sympathy with the poetry.
>
> (Coleridge 1983: 2.15–17)

Following the German idealist philosophy of Kant and Friedrich Schiller, Coleridge argues for an extraordinary authorial balancing act, for a juggling of a number of oppositions within the 'organic' figure of the poet. But what is perhaps remarkable about this description of the 'ideal' poet and what is exemplary of its expression of a 'Romantic' sense of the author is the extent to which the individual, the poet or author, is figured as both at the centre of the definition of poetry and at its margins. The passage asserts the connection of poetry with the individual's 'faculties', with his will, imagination and understanding. But at the same time Coleridge makes it clear that the poet's power is 'magical', that his 'control' is 'gentle and unnoticed' and that 'our admiration for the poet' is subordinate to our 'sympathy with the poetry'. Both there and not there, the poet has a seemingly supernatural, an apparitional or phantasmatic, quality.

LITERARY COMPOSITION

Rather than a stable and coherent theory, the Romantic-expressive conception of authorship is impelled by the contradictions within its own idea of composition. In particular, the Romantics position the author as at the centre of the literary institution by insisting on the immediacy and spontaneity of poetic creation, on the work of art as the direct representation of the creative experience. But this insistence on immediacy may be understood to be a result of its very impossibility. Such, at least, is Friedrich Schiller's point in his influential essay 'On Naive and Sentimental Poetry' (1795–6). In this essay, Schiller contrasts the ancient, 'naive' poet who simply and purely 'follows nature and feeling' with the modern or 'sentimental' (or 'romantic') poet who '*reflects* upon the impression that objects make upon him'. For Schiller, it is only in this alienated, mediated act of reflection that poetry for the modern or 'romantic' poet is constituted (Schiller 1988: 161). In this sense, at least in its formulation within the Romantic tradition, the expressive theory of poetry is more complex, more divided and unstable than Barthes's or even Foucault's attacks on it might suggest. Or to put it differently, the theory of authorship that is deconstructed in poststructuralist theory is, in its prime instance, already undermined by its own irreducible internal tensions. The Romantic-expressive theory of authorship, indeed, contains within itself its own refutation. If Romanticism figures the author as expressing her own ideas, thoughts, volitions, that is to say, it also figures the literary work as being involved in or indeed as constituting an alienated reflection on itself and at the same time, and thereby, as transcending those originating ideas and volitions.

If immediacy is a problem for the Romantic theory of authorship, it is so not least because of the desire for but impossibility of capturing the moment of composition. Indeed, it may be no exaggeration to say that Romantic poetry and poetics are energized precisely by the paradoxical nature of their conception of writing. In his Preface to the second edition of *Lyrical Ballads* (1800), for example, William Wordsworth famously presents an account of the act of composition. 'All good poetry', he declares, 'is the spontaneous overflow of powerful feelings' (Wordsworth 1984: 598). The declaration is emphasized and complicated when Wordsworth returns to the question of poetic spontaneity several pages further on in the Preface:

> I have said that Poetry is the spontaneous overflow of powerful feelings: it takes its origin from emotion recollected in tranquillity: the emotion is contemplated till by a species of reaction the tranquillity disappears, and an emotion kindred to that which was before the subject of contemplation, is gradually produced, and does itself actually exist in the mind. In this mood successful composition generally begins, and in a mood similar to this it is carried on.

> (p. 611)

Wordsworth suggests that while the 'overflow of powerful feelings' that constitutes poetry is 'spontaneous', it is also, and at the same time, not spontaneous. The emotion is 'recollected' and 'contemplated' rather than immediately acted upon or written about. The 'origin' of poetry, therefore, is at one remove from the 'emotion' that the poet experiences. But in order to ameliorate this discrepancy, in order to minimize or even eliminate the deferral involved in composition, Wordsworth goes on to suggest that in fact the poetic act of contemplation itself *produces* an emotion. This emotion is both 'kindred' to the original and 'actually exist[s] in the mind'. In other words, the emotion produced in the poetic act of contemplation is both a copy and itself original. In his complex, guarded and finally contradictory analysis, then, Wordsworth seeks to explain poetry both in terms of the author's experience or emotion and in terms of a supplement to or copy of that experience or emotion – a supplement that finally takes the place of the original. The poem is both a spontaneous overflow and the result of tranquil contemplation. And its *origin*, what it represents or supplements, is precisely that uncannily complicated but very personal emotion, an emotion that is both a copy of an emotion and an authentic, original emotion in itself. It is, in the end, by means of this elaborate, difficult and contradictory logic that the author is placed at the centre of the new, the modern institution of literature.

NOT MYSELF

'Romantic poets are driven to a quest for self-creation and self-comprehension that is unprecedented in literary history', comments Marlon Ross in his study of the formulation of this sense of self-creation within the context of its anxious and urgent masculinity (Ross 1989: 22). And yet, if a defining element in the Romantic invention of the modern sense of authorship is the self-creative and self-centring genius, a defining element in the notion of genius is a certain evacuation of selfhood, the genius's own ignorance or inability or ineffectuality – what John Keats memorably names 'negative capability' (Keats 1958: 1.193). Writing in around 1775, the French writer and encyclopaedist Denis Diderot wittily summed up this sense of the poet's ignorance of his own work when he declared that poetry 'supposes an exaltation of the brain that comes, one could almost say, from divine inspiration. The poet', Diderot continues, 'has profound ideas without knowing their cause or their effects. The philosopher, in whom these same ideas are the fruit of long meditation, is amazed at this, and exclaims: Who inspired so much wisdom in that maniac?' (quoted in Bénichou 1999: 31). Along with classical notions of inspiration expressed in such texts as Plato's *Ion* and Longinus's *On the Sublime* (first century AD), such ideas had enormous influence on the work of Percy Bysshe Shelley. In his *A Defence of Poetry* (written in 1821), Shelley argues that ignorance both is and fundamentally is not intrinsic to poetry, to the work of the poet. Responding to Thomas Love Peacock's declaration in 'The Four Ages of Poetry' (1820) that modern poets are 'wallowing in the rubbish of departed ignorance' (Peacock 1987: 208), Shelley declares both that poetry is the 'centre and circumference of knowledge', and that it is 'not subject to the controul of the active powers of the mind' and has 'no necessary connexion with consciousness or will' (Shelley 1977: 503, 506). Poets, Shelley says, are themselves 'the most sincerely astonished' at their own work, 'hierophants' as they are of an '*un*apprehended inspiration', their words expressing 'what they understand *not*' (p. 508; italics added). Shelley's declaration of poetic independence serves to resurrect and radicalize the ancient tradition of the poet as irrational, crazed or inspired: he is responding, not least, to Socrates' declaration in *Ion* that the poet is 'an airy thing, winged and holy' who is unable to compose 'until he becomes inspired and goes out of his mind and his intellect is no longer in him'.

While Romantic poetry and poetics celebrate the individuality of the author or genius, then, they also assert the essence of genius to be an ability to transcend the self, to go beyond that of which any mortal, fallible individual is capable. The poet, Keats declares in a letter of 1818, is 'not itself – it has no self – it is every thing and nothing – It has no character': the poet is 'the most unpoetical of any thing in existence; because he has no Identity'. The letter is also a declaration of vocation and Keats explains how, when he is in a room full of people, 'if ever I am free from speculating on creations of my own brain, then not myself goes home to myself' and that he is 'in a very little time annihilated' (Keats 1958: 1.387). Similarly, in a very Keatsian discussion of Shakespeare as a 'myriad-minded' poet (Coleridge 1983: 2.19), Coleridge argues that one of the 'promises of genius' is the 'choice of subjects very remote from the private interests and circumstances of the writer himself': 'where the subject is taken immediately from the author's personal sensations and experiences', Coleridge speculates, 'the excellence of a particular poem is but an equiv-ocal mark, and often a fallacious pledge, of genuine poetic power' (p. 20). It is, he goes on, a poet's 'alienation', his '*aloofness*', that marks him out (p. 22). As Coleridge comments elsewhere, 'Genius may co-exist with wildness, idleness, folly, even with crime; but not long, believe me, with selfishness' (Coleridge 1983: 1.33, n.1). What this adds up to is the central paradox of Romantic authorship, one that will haunt poetry, criticism and even literary theory well into the twentieth century. The paradox is that while Romantic poetics focus on authorship, they also evacuate authorship of subjectivity. It is precisely in this way that the Kantian idea of disinterestedness is in fact expressed. The 'autonomy' of the artwork relies on the autonomy of the artist, a paradoxical autonomy in which the author both is and is not himself.

THE ROMANTIC LEGACY

One of the problems with debates concerning the death, life, resurrection and rebirth of the author that have raged in literary theory and criticism since the late 1960s is their unsatisfactory polarization: either the author is, or should be, dead, or she is alive; either the author is present or she is absent; either authorial intention is accessible, relevant, authoritative, or it is superfluous and anyway inaccessible; either we should attend to the life of the poet or to the work. But once you step outside the strict confines of the circular and exclusive terms of this debate you find that since at least the late eighteenth century, writers and critics have almost obsessively dwelled on the complex interaction of authorial presence and absence, on the way that the *centrality* of the author is bound up with, is caused by and a cause of, his or her *marginality*, that authorship indeed is in thrall to the apparitional. We might think, for example, of Keats's fascination with the nature of his own poetic vocation but also with his sense of the poet as 'camelion' and 'the most unpoetical of all God's creatures' (Keats 1958: 1.387). Or we might think of the discourse of the sublime, which puts the poet at the centre of aesthetic discussion while at the same time removing or annulling his or her autonomy and authority within an experience of divine afflatus, of inspiration. This paradox or tension is summed up in Shelley's declaration that poets are the 'hierophants of an unapprehended inspiration', creatures who produce words 'which express what they understand not' and who 'feel not what they inspire' (Shelley 1977: 508).

This paradox is only intensified in late nineteenth and early twentieth-century concentrations on the 'impersonality' of the artist or author. If Romanticism's insistence on the subjectivity of the authorial self also necessarily involves an articulation of an absence or disappearance of the self, the modernists' insistence on impersonality can easily be read in terms of its own subversion, in terms of the return, within authorial impersonality, of the self, the subjectivity of the individual author. An insistence on impersonality, then, also necessarily locks personality securely if paradoxically in place. We can see this, for example, in some much-quoted comments by Flaubert, Eliot and Joyce on the fundamental absence or 'impersonality' of the author or artist. The 'rage', as Henry James puts it, for the idea of impersonality is a 'constant refrain' in Flaubert's letters (James 1981: 138): 'May I be skinned alive before I ever turn my private feelings to literary account', Flaubert declares (quoted in ibid.). Most famously, perhaps, Flaubert declares in a letter of March 1857 that 'The artist in his work must be like God in his creation', going on to define the uncanny nature of authorial presence as 'invisible and all-powerful'. The artist, Flaubert proposes, 'must be everywhere felt, but never seen' (Flaubert 1980: 230). The declaration is incorporated into Stephen Dedalus's egocentric assertion in James Joyce's *Portrait of the Artist as a Young Man* that the 'personality of the artist . . . finally refines itself out of existence, impersonalises itself' and that the artist, 'like the God of creation, remains within or behind or beyond or above his handiwork, invisible, refined out of existence, indifferent, paring his fingernails' (Joyce 2000: 180–1). But Flaubert and Joyce remind us, even in their declarations of the impersonality of the artist, of the egocentricity of the modern – the post-medieval and especially the Romantic – artist. As D.C. Greetham puts it, Joyce, like Flaubert, presents a figure who is the 'creator of a material universe over which he has complete control at the moment of conception but from which type he is absent . . . in its present, corrupted traces' (Greetham 1999: 30). So it is no surprise to find that precisely such egocentricity is at the heart of what W.K. Wimsatt identifies as T.S Eliot's 'highly ambiguous' and indeed 'seminally confused' essay 'Tradition and the Individual Talent' (Wimsatt 1976: 119, 122). The essay was first published in 1919 in an avant-garde journal edited by Ezra Pound and named, significantly enough, *The Egotist: An Individual Review*. In it, Eliot famously and influentially mounted an attack on the Romantic conception of the personalized author by making the arch-Romantic declaration that the 'progress of an artist' involves 'a continual self-sacrifice, a continual extinction of personality' and asserting that 'No poet, no artist of any art, has his complete meaning alone' (Eliot 1975: 40, 38). Similarly, in a rather less well-known declaration in *The Use of Poetry and the Use of Criticism*, Eliot argued against judging poetry by reference to its 'putative antecedents in the mind of the poet' (quoted in Wimsatt 1976: 119). But if poetry is, as he puts it in his famous essay, not a 'turning loose of emotion, but an escape from emotion; not the expression of personality but an escape from personality', Eliot also reminds us that 'only those who have personality and emotions know what it means to want to escape' from them (Eliot 1975: 43). Eliot's suffering, 'self-sacrificing' artist is none other than the Romantic genius, sacrificing himself to his art but in so doing creating or revealing himself in and at the centre of that art. The chronically autobiographical W.B. Yeats in fact displays a somewhat similar ambivalence when he opens a 1937 essay on his own work by declaring that 'A poet writes always of his personal life' but that he 'never speaks directly as to someone at the breakfast table' since 'there is always a phantasmagoria'. 'Even when the poet seems most himself', Yeats declares, 'he is never the bundle of accidents and incoherence that sits down to breakfast; he has been re-born as an idea, something intended, completed: the writer is 'part of his own phantasmagoria' (Yeats 1994: 204).

Much twentieth-century thinking around the question of authorship does in fact seem to insist on the disappearance, irrelevance or incoherence of the author. As Douglas Dunn comments, 'Self-annihilation and "impersonality" . . . have become chimeras after which some poets choose to hunt' (Dunn 2000: 165): 'It is my ambition to be, as a private individual, abolished and voided from history', writes William Faulkner in 1949, 'leaving it markless, no refuse save the printed books. . . . It is my aim . . . that the sum and history of my life, which in the same sentence is my obit and epitaph too, shall be them both: He made the books and he died' (Faulkner 1977: 285). Faulkner might have been thinking of Flaubert's comment that 'The artist must so arrange things that posterity will not believe he ever lived' (quoted in Wood 1994: 11). 'Anonymity, of some real if not literal sort, is a condition of poetry', opines John Crowe Ransom, writing in 1938: 'A good poem, even if it is signed with a full and well-known name, intends as a work of art to lose the identity of the author' (Ransom 1968: 2). The comments echo E.M. Forster's forthright idea, expressed in a 1925 essay, that 'all literature tends towards a condition of anonymity' (Forster 1951: 92).

In particular, twentieth-century writers' versions of the author often seem peculiarly concerned to resist that figure's authority. The author as unknowing, as not, or as not quite, conscious of what she does, as impersonal or as multiple, are perhaps the most common forms of twentieth- and indeed twenty-first-century authors' explanations of their own work. Such writers often echo Eliot's declaration that the poet doesn't 'have' 'his complete meaning alone'. 'For me the initial delight is in the surprise of remembering something I didn't know I knew', Robert Frost says of the process of writing (Frost 2000: 45). 'I feel that, in a sense, the writer knows nothing any longer', J.G. Ballard comments in his 1974 Introduction to the French edition of *Crash* (1973) (Ballard 1990: 9). One of the consequences of such thinking is that interpretation should therefore be left to others: 'The author of a poem is not necessarily the ideal person to explain its meaning', Robert Lowell comments, since the poet is 'as liable as anyone else to muddle, dishonesty, and reticence' and has no particularly privileged perspective on the matter. For Lowell himself, at least, what 'I didn't intend often seems now at least as valid as what I did' (Lowell 2000: 106–7). Such statements of poetic ignorance or of un- or non-intentionality or contingency are pervasive in twentieth-century poetics: 'In the very essence of poetry there is something indecent: / a thing is brought forth which we didn't know we had in us', says Czeslaw Milosz in 'Ars Poetica' (Milosz 1979: 3). 'I don't know who I am, what soul I have. . . . The human author of these books does not recognize in himself any personality', confides the irrepressibly multiple Portuguese poet Fernando Pessoa in one of his guises, as the poet Fernando Pessoa (Pessoa 1979: 5–7). 'While there is nothing automatic about the poem', Wallace Stevens declares of 'The Old Woman and the Statue' in an appropriately tangled passage from his essay 'The Irrational Element in Poetry' (*c.*1937),

> nevertheless it has an automatic aspect in the sense that it is what I wanted it to be without knowing before it was written what I wanted it to be, even though I knew before it was written what I wanted to do. If each of us is a biological mechanism, each poet is a poetic mechanism. To the extent that what he produces is mechanical: that is to say, beyond his power to change, it is irrational. Perhaps I do not mean wholly beyond his power to change for he might, by an effort of the will, change it. With that in mind, I mean beyond likelihood of change so long as he is being himself.
>
> (Stevens 1979: 50–1)

The poem, Charles Simic comments, 'mostly writes itself' (quoted in Weberman 2002: 64); 'The poet does not write what he knows but what he does not know', concurs W.S. Graham (2000: 119). 'Writing reveals to you what you wanted to say in the first place', remarks J.M. Coetzee: 'In fact, it sometimes constructs what you want or wanted to say. . . . Writing shows or creates . . . what your desire was, a moment ago' (quoted in Attridge 2004: 23). Dwelling on the reception of his poetry in the Introduction to *Other Traditions*, John Ashbery comments, bemusedly, that while there appears to be agreement in the academic world that 'there's something interesting about my poetry', there is at the same time 'little agreement as to its ultimate worth and considerable confusion about what, if anything, it means'. And he comments that people often ask why, if he can 'invent poetry', he can't 'invent meaning', offering as a kind of justification W.H. Auden's remark that 'If I could tell you, I would let you know' (Ashbery 2000: 1–2).

But these assertions of authorial ignorance and absence should be understood as the other side of the modernist and postmodernist coin of personality. The twentieth century was indeed the era of the literary confession, of the literary memoir, of self-exposure and revelation, not only in the so-called 'confessional' poets Sylvia Plath, Robert Lowell, John Berryman and others, but also in the pervasive sense that an author somehow expresses something of herself in her writing. Again, examples of writers talking about this 'confessional' impulse, this confessional poetic, are not difficult to find, and indeed one of the functions that many contemporary writers readily accept is that of interviewee, memoirist or autobiographer of their own writing lives. 'Writers – the writers I most admire at any rate – make some use of their own lives', comments Raymond Carver (1988: 16). 'It is amazing', Charles Taylor remarks, 'how much art in the twentieth century has itself for its subject, or is on one level at least thinly disguised allegory about the artist and his work' (Taylor 1989: 481). Almost every major writer of the twentieth century seems to have produced a memoir or literary autobiography: Joseph Conrad's *The Mirror and the Sea* (1906) and *A Personal Record* (1912); Henry James's *A Small Boy and Others* (1913), *Notes of a Son and Brother* (1914) and *The Middle Years* (dictated 1914); Thomas Hardy's ghost-written 'Life' (1928, 1930); Virginia Woolf's *A Sketch of the Past* (written 1939–40); W.B. Yeats's *Autobiographies* (1955); Jean Rhys's *Smile Please* (1979); Vladimir Nabokov's *Speak Memory* (1967); Janet Frame's three-part *Autobiography* (1991); Doris Lessing's *Under My Skin* (1994); J.M. Coetzee's *Boyhood:*

Scenes from Provincial Life (1997), to name a few. But what Romanticism allows us to understand is that such confessionalism is not incompatible with impersonality, that autobiography can be a way of depersonalizing, of disowning, the self, just as the project of impersonality can be bound up with an expression of an intense subjectivity.

The lasting poetic inheritance of Romanticism, then, has been a paradoxical one in which the author is seen as both central to the institution of literature and evacuated or voided from that institution. The paradox has two consequences in particular. First: the Romantic author is always a fiction. The Romantic conception of authorship involves an ideal, an impossible ideal, of autonomy. While the Romantic author is seen as self-originating and original in a fundamental, radical sense, as wholly detached from social context, just the fact that she uses language, exploits certain genres, and operates within certain literary traditions and with certain conceptual and poetic conventions, determines her as an unequivocally social being. Indeed, the very gesture of inauguration, of originality, is itself a literary convention: to be 'original' in this respect is to be precisely *un*original. Second: the Romantic author is a fiction in the sense that the notion of the autonomous author described above is itself only part of the sense of authorship developed by early nineteenth-century poets and critics. Romanticism itself does not simply involve the celebration of the originating autonomous genius, since it only does so within a context in which such a figure is at the same time subverted. Indeed, the Romantic 'ideology' of authorship, conceived as a homogeneous, self-consistent body of theory, may well speak more to our own needs than to those of the Romantics, may well be a 'twentieth-century construct designed for polemical and anti-Romantic purposes' (Ruthven 2001: 91). The Romantic author is, in a sense, a fiction of subsequent critical reception, a fantasy, a back-formation or 'retrojection' produced through a partial reading of Romantic poetics since in fact Romantic thinking around authorship is precisely constituted in and by conflict, paradox, instability. In this regard, in as much as the whole project of contemporary literary theory is often thought to be promulgated on the proposition of the 'death' of the (Romantic) author, it may be said to be chasing shadows, and may itself be a will-o'-the-wisp, a chimera.

4

FORMALISM, FEMINISM, HISTORICISM

Since its inception in the nineteenth century, literary studies in its professional or academic mode and as it is taught at universities in Europe and North America has been dominated by debates over the nature and the status of the author and indeed over the legitimacy of addressing issues of authorship at all. The question of the author may even be conceived, as it is by Seán Burke, in terms not only of a question in literary theory but as '*the* question of theory' (Burke 1998: 191, italics added). In other words, the way that authorship is understood may be said to define literary theory, and therefore to determine the way that literature and reading itself are conceived. In this chapter, I will briefly survey three major strands in twentieth-century literary criticism and theory – formalism, feminism, and new historicism – in order to indicate ways in which the question of the author is fundamental to such thinking about literature, literary criticism and literary theory, even when it seems not to be. The author, we might say, is an inescapable factor in criticism and theory, not least when she is most firmly being pronounced dead.

FORMALISM

Professional academic criticism emerged in the late nineteenth and twentieth centuries out of the disciplines of rhetoric, philology, literary history, and literary editing, all of which have their own distinctive relationships with the question of the author. Academic criticism as such may be said to have been born out of a reaction against the idea that the author stands at the centre of the work of literary interpretation. The professionalization and institutionalization of literary studies, of criticism in particular, as a rigorous, scholarly discipline, and as distinct from rhetoric, philology, literary history and biography, and literary editing, involved, at least in theory, a self-conscious purging of the leisurely, dilettante pursuit of literature, and of forms of connoisseurship in which questions of biography, psycho-biography, and authorial intention dominated. Indeed, much of the *resistance* to the introduction of English Literature as a university subject arose out of the sense that the study of literature would amount, at most, to a form of the higher gossip, to 'chatter about Shelley', that such a discipline would be irredeemably tainted by a concern with the trivial and mystificatory personalism of biography. As the critic Walter Raleigh put it at the beginning of the twentieth century, 'the main business of criticism' was to 'raise the dead' (quoted in Baldick 1983: 78). Writing in 1869, for example, Alexander Bain, Professor of Logic and English Literature at the University of Aberdeen, argued that the teaching of English in universities should be restricted to the study of rhetoric or of what we would now call 'composition', since

> when a man gets into literary criticism at large, the temptation to deviate into matters that have no value for the predominating end of a teacher of English, is far beyond the lure of alcohol, tobacco, or any sensual stimulation. He runs into digressions on the life, the character, the likings and dislikings, the quarrels and the friendships of his authors; and even gets involved in their doctrines and controversies.
>
> (Bain 1869: 213–14)

Writing from a very different perspective and from a very different cultural, political and national context in 1921, the Russian formalist critic and linguist Roman Jakobson is equally scathing about the temptation of the biographical in literary criticism. Like Bain, Jakobson deploys a melodramatic metaphor to delineate his sense of traditional literary history. 'Historians of literature', he declares, 'act like nothing so much as police-men, who, out to arrest a certain culprit, take into custody (just in case) everything and everyone they find at the scene as well as any passers-by for good measure'. Such critics or 'historians', he argues, have 'helped themselves to everything – environment, psychology, politics, philosophy' and in so doing have developed their own 'concoction of homemade disciplines' (quoted in Eichenbaum 1998: 8). As Paul de Man remarks, in the context of a discussion of the formalism of Michael Riffaterre, literary texts 'do not quite know what it is that they are talking about' in the sense that 'whenever one is supposed to speak of literature, one speaks of anything under the sun . . . except literature': the formalist circum-scription of literature, he remarks, is constituted as 'a way to safeguard a discipline which constantly threatens to degenerate into gossip, trivia or self-obsession' (de Man 1986: 29).

The academic study of literature dominant in the middle decades of the twentieth century therefore conceived of itself in terms of its resistance to what was seen as the unprofessional and unscholarly rehearsal of, in particular, the gossip of biography and biographical or psychological interpretation. The overlapping schools of formalism and new criticism were both concerned to examine in detail the workings of 'the words on the page'. In this respect, formalists and new critics were concerned above all with a certain purity, with a desire for the purification of criticism, and this purification involved, in particular, the rejection of questions of authorship as pertinent to interpretation. The sense that attending to authors' lives can easily slide into literary gossip is suggested by the case of Shakespeare's *Sonnets*, a work that famously raises troubling questions of authorship. 'That there is so little genuine criticism in the terrifying number of books and essays on Shakespeare's sonnets', L.C. Knights begins a 1934 essay, 'can only be partly accounted for by the superior attractiveness of gossip' (Knights 1946: 40). Such a concern with the possibility that talk about the sonnets will turn into gossip about Shakespeare's life spans the twentieth century, in fact: writing in the Introduction to his 1986 edition of Shakespeare's poems, John Kerrigan comments that 'biographical reading . . . has so little purchase' on Shakespeare's poems that 'criticism directed along such lines soon finds itself spinning off the text into vacuous literary chit-chat' (Kerrigan 1986: 11; see Burrow 1998: 44). Both Knights and Kerrigan, in their different ways, share at least some of the characteristics of 'new' or 'formalist' criticism, criticism that was conceived as rigorously and exclusively literary, that was language-based and text-bound, and that makes the literary text its 'central concern' (Brooks 1998: 52). Indeed, ever vigilant for the lurking temptations, the tempting addictions, of biography and of 'psychological' interpretation, one of the major concerns of formalism and new criticism is to establish a clear demarcation between work and life.

In 'The Formalist Critics' (1951), Cleanth Brooks, one of the major spokesmen for American New Criticism, attempted to construct a clear division of 'the work itself' from 'speculation on the mental processes of the author'. The problem with such speculation, Brooks argues, is that it 'takes the critic away from the work into biography and psychology', and while an account of the biography or psychology of the writer is 'very much worth making', he suggests, it 'should not be confused with an account of the work' (Brooks 1998: 53). Brooks concedes that there is nothing wrong with biography and psychology, so long as it is kept in its place, and out of academic criticism. But as with Bain, Knight, Kerrigan and others, Brooks can't help using phrases like 'trivial', 'literary gossip' and 'literary chit chat', and 'talking about literature for the hell of it' to describe the kind of literary analysis that involves reference to the life, opinions, thoughts and intentions of the author. The critic has a 'specific job as a critic', Brooks declares, and that job is to attend to the work itself rather than to these unprofessional, trivial and essentially (we might surmise) discreditably *feminine* aspects of literary discussion (Brooks 1998: 53–5).

A similar attempt to separate the life from the work was central to an essay published some five years before Brooks's, one that was to become one of the most influential statements in Anglo-American literary studies in the twentieth century, W.K. Wimsatt and Monroe C. Beardsley's 'The Intentional Fallacy' (1946). The impulse behind the essay, the desire to purge literary criticism of the indiscipline of the alleged 'femininity' of gossip, the impulse to discipline literary studies, was made clear in later essays written as clarifications and modifications of the original ground-breaking piece. In these later statements, both Wimsatt and Beardsley separately explain that, like Brooks, they were concerned about the muddled, gossipy indulgence of much that went on in the name of English literary studies. In a 1976 essay, Wimsatt remarks that 'The Intentional Fallacy' had been directed against 'the flux, the gossip, the muddle and the "motley"' that, he says, constituted literary criticism at the time (Wimsatt 1976: 137); while in an article from 1982, Beardsley comments that the original essay had been written 'for those literary theorists who could no longer put up with the mishmash of philology, biography, moral admonition, textual exegesis, social history, and sheer burbling that largely made up what was thought of as literary criticism' (Beardsley 1982: 188). As both critics make clear, the intention behind 'The Intentional Fallacy' was to try to discipline the 'muddle', the 'mishmash', and the 'sheer burbling' of contemporary literary criticism, to clarify the nature and status of statements about literary texts, to discipline the discipline, to make it austerely literary, rigorously linguistic, and astringently intellectual. And the muddle that Wimsatt and Beardsley discern in mid-century literary studies, the chit chat that Brooks describes, is clearly centred around the question of the messy, contingent and unpredictably complicated personalism of 'the author'.

It is worth looking a little more closely at Wimsatt and Beardsley's famous essay, however, since beneath what appears as the headline rejection of the author there is at work a more complex and in some ways more subtle engagement. As its title suggests, 'The Intentional Fallacy' is not so much about authors as about authorial intention. The essay engages with one of the most important and one of the most troubling questions in any attempt to think about literary texts, the question of whether or not our sense of what a text means should be determined by our sense of what the author meant by it. The answer that Wimsatt and Beardsley give is a resounding 'no'. The major claim of 'The Intentional Fallacy' is that the 'design or intention of the author is neither available nor desirable as a standard for judging the success of a work of literary art' and that there is 'hardly a problem of literary criticism in which the critic's approach will not be qualified by his view of "intention"' (Wimsatt and Beardsley 1954: 3). Wimsatt and Beardsley concede that there is a causal relation between poet and poem – that, as they say, a poem comes 'out of a head, not out of a hat' (p. 4) – but argue that this does not allow us to extrapolate from what we take to be the author's intentions when we judge or interpret a text. In this sense, Wimsatt and Beardsley are not denying that authors have intentions: in fact, they suggest that authorial intention is precisely what gets expressed in and as the words of the text. Indeed, in his later essay, Wimsatt explicitly declares that an artwork and especially a verbal artwork 'is in a sense . . . made of intentions or intentionalistic material', and that 'whatever does get into a poem presumably is put there by the poet' (Wimsatt 1976: 116, 120). But the critic's task, Wimsatt and Beardsley propose, is to understand those intentions *as the text expresses them*. 'How', they ask, can a critic understand 'what the poet tried to do?':

> If the poet succeeded in doing it, then the poem itself shows what he was trying to do. And if the poet did not succeed, then the poem is not adequate evidence, and the critic must go outside the poem – for evidence of an intention that did not become effective in the poem.
>
> (Wimsatt and Beardsley 1954: 4)

According to this logic, if an intention does not 'become effective' in the text, it is, by definition, not part of the text. And if it is not part of the text, it is no part of the critic's job to search for or to attend to it. In other words, far from rejecting authorial intention, 'The Intentional Fallacy' embraces it but argues that it just is the literary text, that authorial intention just is the meaning of that particular form of words.

The simplistic dismissal of authorship, of authorial intention, that has often seemed to be the legacy of Wimsatt and Beardsley's essay, amounts therefore to something of a misreading. Wimsatt and Beardsley are concerned to suggest that intentions are complicated things, that they certainly exist, that they are expressed by the text itself, but that the task of the critic is to attend to the evidence of the text without regard to 'extrinsic' matters such as the *extra-textual* thoughts, wishes, desires, experiences, life or indeed the imagined or separately documented 'intentions' of the author. They also concede that this separation is often more difficult than it might seem. And it is one of the ironies of literary history that what we might conceive of as Wimsatt and Beardsley's own intentions, as they are expressed in their essay, have often been misconstrued, and that, as Wendell Harris comments, the essay is usually seen as dismissing altogether 'the relevance or possibility of discovering authorially intended meaning'. As a result, Harris comments, a whole generation of students and scholars have tried 'as hard as possible to avoid all reference to authorial intention' (Harris 1996: 95–6). This has led to some frankly bizarre ideas about literary interpretation: the idea, for example, that we should discuss, say, the poetry of Sylvia Plath or Robert Lowell without reference to the way in which those poets' work is constructed around a certain configuration of their lives; or the idea that we should interpret the speaker's declaration in T.S. Eliot's *The Waste Land* (his 'personal . . . grouse against life', as Eliot himself called it) that 'On Margate Sands. / I can connect / Nothing with nothing' (ll. 300–2), with, as a matter of principle, no reference whatsoever to the fact that in the autumn of 1921 Eliot went to Margate to recover from, or to experience, a breakdown as well as to continue writing his poem. The fact that, in this example, such an event in Eliot's life might tell us little about other aspects of the poem, and the properly conceived resistance to the sense that literary texts are all too often limited by or indeed limited to a certain sentimental identification with the author's life, has led critics to perform acts of extraordinary self-denial in the name of a scrupulous textualism (or 'formalism'). But it might be argued that, to take just a couple more examples, reading John Donne's poems as verbal icons isolated from the coterie context of their composition will produce at best a partial reading (see Marotti 1986); or that overlooking Edmund Spenser's involvement in the colonial government that brutally repressed the Irish in the latter half of the sixteenth century will itself lead to a distorted understanding, a misreading of *The Faerie Queene* (see Hadfield 1997). Most notoriously, though, what we might see as rigidly anti-authorial misreadings can work the other way round: for several centuries there was, as one strategy for reading Shakespeare's sonnets, a concerted attempt by writers and critics clearly to separate the author from the poems because of the shocking possibility that the evident homoeroticism of the sonnets would inexorably lead to the conclusion that the bard himself was queer.

Wimsatt and Beardsley's essay had, then, enormous and in some ways unpredictable consequences for the academic study of literature in the decades after its first publication. But it was also subject to vigorous challenges by, for example, E.D. Hirsch in *Validity in Interpretation* (1967) and *The Aims of Interpretation* (1976) and, more recently, William Irwin in his updating of Hirsch's books in *Intentionalist Interpretation* (1999). Hirsch's basic argument is that there is an important distinction to be maintained between the 'meaning' of a work and its 'significance'. For

Hirsch, the meaning of the work is indeed bound up with what the author intended by it, while the work's 'significance', what he defines as 'any perceived relationship between construed verbal meaning and something else' (Hirsch 1967: 140), may or may not be confined by, indeed may or may not be related to, those intentions. Against Wimsatt and Beardsley's assertion that the 'meaning' of a text just is that which inheres in the text itself, Hirsch declares that if a text 'means what it says, then it means nothing in particular', since its meaning must be 'construed' in relation to the original intention of the author (p. 13). While Wimsatt and Beardsley seem to equate meaning with language, with the words of the text, Hirsch argues that there is no sense in declaring meaning to be a function of language since it is necessarily 'an affair of consciousness' rather than of the 'physical signs of things' (p. 23). For Hirsch, the idea that 'linguistic signs can somehow speak their own meaning' is 'a mystical idea that has never been persuasively defended' (p. 23). But while meaning is fixed, and while it is in principle objectively verifiable by reference to the author's intentions, Hirsch argues that 'significance', by contrast, is in principle whatever a reader might choose to make of it. He argues that there is 'literally no limit to the significance of the shortest and most banal text', since significance can include 'all conceivable states of affairs – historical, linguistic, psychological, physical, metaphysical, personal, familial, national' – and can even encompass 'changing conditions in all conceivable states of affairs' at different times (p. 63).

For Wimsatt and Beardsley, then, authorial intention is a legitimate focus for interpretation just to the extent that it is articulated in or expressed by the text itself. For E.D. Hirsch, by contrast, non-intentional 'significance' is a legitimate focus for interpretation just so long as it is acknowledged that the essential *meaning* of a text, the very ground-work of any interpretation, has been previously established in relation to what the author intended. In fact, though, both sides of this apparently unbridgeable dispute make such major concessions as to suggest that their positions may not be quite as implacably opposed as they might seem. For their part, Wimsatt and Beardsley concede that it is not always easy or indeed in practice possible to distinguish between 'internal' and 'external' aspects of a text and that a text just is an expression of an author's intentions. For his part, Hirsch allows, as 'significance', the validity of non-intentional, non-authorized interpretations. In so doing, Hirsch may be thought to have opened the 'floodgates' (see Wimsatt 1976: 121) of interpretation since there is almost nothing that can in principle be excluded from the category of 'significance'. Moreover, when an intentionalist theorist like William Irwin declares that 'Whatever the author intended to communicate is the meaning of the text' (Irwin 2002b: 199), he can sound uncannily like Wimsatt and Beardsley, who would presumably be happy with such a formulation just so long as the emphasis was on the word 'text'.

Although Steven Knapp argues that 'one of the main intuitions underlying the various forms of literary formalism' is the idea that 'the meaning of the work goes beyond what its author intended' (Knapp 1993: 5–6), there is a sense that, in this debate over intentions, Wimsatt and Beardsley on the one hand and Hirsch on the other agree that the author intends something and that, in different ways, interpretation should be limited by those intentions. What neither party allows for is the possibility that the work of writing involves, precisely, going beyond the conscious intentions of the writing subject, that the writing subject, at some point, somewhere, in some sense, doesn't know what she is doing. This may be related to the fact that between 1940 and 1997 there was no major study in English of one of the most important, if in some senses one of the most scandalous, even disreputable, conceptions of authorship in the Western tradition, the tradition of the poet as inspired, since inspiration involves the scandalous transcendence of authorial intention (see Clark 1997: 1–2 and *passim*). But as I have tried to suggest in Chapter 3, above, this quality of not knowing is intrinsic to many authors' own conceptions of what they are doing. By contrast, both Wimsatt/Beardsley and Hirsch seem to rely on an assumption about authorial communication, the assumption that authors can be fully conscious, fully *intentional* with regard to the meanings that they seek to communicate. It is an assumption, indeed, about communication itself. But as Jason Holt has noted, this notion of literature as communication seems to sit badly with the experience of reading literary texts. Kafka's *The Trial*, Holt points out, is 'a terribly inefficient means of conveying the idea that life is bureaucratically oppressive, implacably irrational, and irremediably bleak' (Holt 2002: 71). Indeed, as Holt implies, however unlovely it is, his own sentence is, in this regard, far more efficient than is Kafka's novel. We might therefore be inclined to conclude that what is literary about *The Trial* may just be its inefficiency in conveying this or any other 'message'. Another, rather different, objection to this fundamental premise of debates over intentionalism is summed up by Richard Rorty's comment on Martin Heidegger's work in the context of that philosopher's National Socialist sympathies. The solution to the problem that one of the great European philosophers of the twentieth century was also actively involved in the Nazi cause in the 1930s and failed even until his death in 1976 clearly to condemn that cause or to distance his later self from the beliefs and actions of the younger man is, Rorty suggests, 'to read his books as he would not have wished them to be read', which means, in Heidegger's case, 'in a cool hour, with curiosity, and an open, tolerant mind' (Rorty 1995: 299). In some cases at least, Rorty suggests, the best way to understand the meaning of a work is precisely to overlook, disown, resist, disregard, forget or ignore the author and his or her intentions. To return to literature, the point can be summed up by quoting Shoshana Felman's remarks to the effect that a 'great' literary text is literary precisely to the extent that it is 'self-transgressive' in relation to the 'conscious ideologies' that inform it (Felman 1993: 6).

A potentially surprising but not unhelpful way to think about these matters would be to consider a brief account of interpretation in a book published in the same year as Hirsch's *Validity in Interpretation*, Jacques Derrida's *Of Grammatology*. In his numerous publications over a period of more than thirty-five years, Derrida has consistently probed questions of identity, presence, responsibility, the name, intentionality, subjectivity, the signature, singularity, and autobiography. As Derrida commented in 1980 of his own work, his writings place 'the greatest . . . emphasis' on questions of

> the rights of property, on copyright, on the signature and the market, on the market for . . . culture and all its representations, on speculation on what is proper, one's own, on the name, on destination and resti-tution, on all the institutional borders and structures of discourses, on the whole machinery of publishing and on the media.
>
> (Derrida 1983: 48–9)

In other words, Derrida's work has consistently revolved around a certain thinking – or rethinking – of authorship and intention. Indeed, his work is deeply invested in an interrogation of the question of the author and may be read in part at least as an investigation of the name and nature, the identity and the institution, of authorship (see, for example, Derrida 1984, especially pp. 20–6). While Derrida is often associated (implicitly, at least, by Michel Foucault, for example) with Barthes's proclamation of the death of the author, he has in fact argued that 'too much of a case has been made' for that 'death or omission' (Derrida 1984: 22) and has repeatedly questioned the kinds of oppositions (such as: text and life; life and death; language and its other; inside and outside; intentionality and non-intentionality) on which Barthes's declaration necessarily depends. Indeed, although it is commonly thought that, as Wendell Harris puts it, 'Derrida dismisses intention' (Harris 1996: 113), in fact he consistently defers to authorial intention as 'a crucial element in any critical reading' (Royle 2003: 56). At the same time, Derrida's work is concerned, in Peggy Kamuf's words, with 'the gap through which conscious, finite, selfsame intentions risk being detached from their meaning' and with the 'otherness that necessarily inhabits and makes possible any intention' (Kamuf 1988: 189).

Derrida's work is pervasively engaged with the apparent paradox that an author can always say 'more, less, or something other than what he *would mean* [*voudrait dire*]' (Derrida 1976: 158). In a well-known section of *Of Grammatology* in which he tries to explain his 'principles of reading', Derrida suggests that reading 'must always aim at a certain relationship, unperceived by the writer, between what he commands and what he does not command of the patterns of the language that he uses. This relationship', Derrida continues, is a 'signifying structure that critical reading should *produce*'. He elaborates this point by arguing that reading is not simply a question of 'produc[ing] this signifying structure' by means of a certain reproduction of the text through an 'effaced and respectful doubling of commentary'. The reader cannot *simply* repeat what the text says, cannot simply record the 'conscious, voluntary, intentional' aspect of the text. Derrida grants that the reader cannot do without this 'indispensable guardrail' of faithful reading, since without it one could 'say almost anything'. And yet only to perform or produce such a 'doubling' of the text, he suggests, is to overlook the fact that the writer, the 'presumed subject of the sentence', might say 'more, less, or something other than what he *would mean*' since the writer 'writes *in* a language and *in* a logic whose proper system, laws, and life his discourse by definition cannot dominate absolutely' (Derrida 1976: 157–8). As Derrida comments in 'The Time of a Thesis', 'this is what I hold and what in turn holds me in its grip, the aleatory strategy of someone who admits that he does not know where he is going' (Derrida 1983: 50): 'you can take interest in what I am doing', Derrida declares in *Glas* (1974), 'only insofar as you would be right to believe that – *somewhere* – I do not know what I am doing' (quoted in Kamuf 1988: 125). That, for Derrida, is where reading begins, in that surprise, in that *authorial* ignorance of what is being said. And it is this that the debate over intentionality often overlooks. Indeed, it might be argued that it is just this sense of a fundamental or constitutive uncertainty of authorial intention that distinguishes literature itself from other discourses, from philosophy, say: it may be that our reading of a poem or other literary text *begins*, in a certain sense, when we can believe that we have located something that the author didn't fully, consciously, properly intend, or that she intended only in the blink of an eye, in the periphery of a certain vision.

FEMINISM

As I have suggested, the rhetoric of gossip that seems to characterize the formalist and new critical rejection of biographical and psychological criticism involves an implicit identification of such approaches with femininity. As if in confirmation of this gendering of the discourse of literary authorship, the efflorescence of 'second-generation' feminism which began in the late 1960s was bound up with investigations of the history, psychology and biography of individual authors. Indeed, there is a strong case to be made for the proposition that feminist literary criticism is *inextricably* bound up with questions of authorship just because of the apparently fundamental, apparently immovable fact of the author's sex: as Seán Burke remarks, 'the struggles of feminism have been primarily a struggle for authorship' (Burke 1995: 145). Thus, when it comes to considering the different ways in which men and women are represented in, for example, *Daniel Deronda*, it matters that, despite the disguise of her pen-name, George Eliot was not a man. Similarly, at its most schematic, it matters to Kate Millett, in her ground-breaking polemic *Sexual Politics* (1971), that the author of the irredeemably misogynistic novel *Sons and Lovers* was a man: what difference would it make to Millett's caustic deconstruction of Lawrence's sexual ideology if the author's name had been, say, Davina Henrietta Lawrence? Millett's point is, though, that given the prevailing social conditions, no such novel *could* have been written by a woman. Rather differently, one of the founding texts of twentieth-century feminism, Virginia Woolf's *A Room of One's Own* (1929), is centrally concerned with what it means to be a writer who is a woman and with the question of how a female author can invent a literary tradition for herself, how she can create an identity for herself as an author. And since much of the feminist revolution in literary criticism of the 1970s and 1980s involved an attempt to recover a female literary tradition, to establish a tradition or canon of female authors, feminism may be seen to be concerned, in the first place, with authorship. In the 1970s, Elaine Showalter coined the term 'gynocriticism' to refer to the study of 'women *as writers*', including 'the history, style, themes, genres, and structure of writing by women; the psychodynamics of female creativity; the trajectory of the individual or collective female career; and the evolution and laws of a female literary tradition' (Showalter 1986: 248). More generally, the very project of feminism is commonly identified with the possibility of confirming a certain identity, of elaborating a solidarity as well as organizing a resistance to patriarchy based around gendered identity. In this respect, authorship is, as Rita Felski comments, 'an indispensable part of the feminist toolkit' (Felski 2003: 58).

The question of the author, then, is at the centre of, is intrinsic to, a certain conception of feminist literary criticism. This being the case, some critics perceived a certain inevitability as well as a certain historical irony in a situation whereby just at the time that feminism was beginning to develop a female literary tradition, authors themselves were being declared dead. Nancy K. Miller, for example, argues that the 'removal of the author' can be seen as an attack on the very foundation of feminist discourse, on the politics of identity. The theory of the death of the author, she suggests, far from leading to a new thinking of authorship, instead 'repressed and inhibited discussion of any writing identity' and therefore of the identity, the identification, of female authors (Miller 1995: 195). In fact, though, Miller goes on to suggest that since the theory of the death of the author threatened to 'prematurely foreclose the question of agency' for women and since women had never been coded as possessing the kind of authoritative status claimed by male writers, the theory of the death of the author simply doesn't apply to them:

> Because women have not had the same historical relation of identity to origin, institution, production that men have had, they have not, I think, (collectively) felt burdened by *too much* self, ego, cogito, etc. Because the female subject has juridically been excluded from the polis, hence decentred, 'disoriginated', deinstitutionalised, etc., her relation to integrity and textuality, desire and authority, displays structurally important differences from that universal position.
>
> (p. 197)

In other words, the deconstruction of the author can be seen, in effect, as the deconstruction of the masculine author, part of the deconstruction of a certain thinking of masculinity, of patriarchy itself. After all, as critics have argued, the stress laid on authorship may itself be related to a more general concern amongst men over the question of paternity. In that case, it may not be coincidental that the author's death or disappearance was most forcefully proposed in the late 1960s by two men who in effect challenge such notions of masculinity by being both childless and queer. Few critics have in fact commented in this context on the fact that both Barthes and Foucault were homosexual (one exception being Metz (2003)), perhaps because to do so would be precisely to risk the crude reductiveness of an *ad hominem* argument that would seem naively to ignore the complexity of the critiques of subjectivity embedded within those theorists' work. But as far as a certain thinking of femininity and feminism is concerned, far from constituting an oppressive authority in need of dismantling or deconstruction, the female author was seen as needing to be constructed, to be affirmed, to be identified, to be given an identity.

The title of one of the most influential books in Anglo-American feminist criticism, Sandra Gilbert and Susan Gubar's *The Madwoman in the Attic* (1979), sets out to construct just such an identity and itself points to the importance of the relationship between feminist criticism and authorship. The word 'Madwoman' in Gilbert and Gubar's title applies equally to female characters in nineteenth-century texts (to Bertha Mason, in the first place, the madwoman imprisoned in an attic in Charlotte

Brontë's *Jane Eyre*), and to nineteenth-century female authors, who are seen as trapped and indeed maddened by their (non-)place in patriarchal society and in the male literary canon. In this respect, Gilbert and Gubar's book is exemplary of a certain tradition of feminist criticism and of the attempt to configure a female literary tradition. The problem that Gilbert and Gubar address centres on the way that for women writers 'the essential process of self-definition is complicated by all those patriarchal definitions that intervene between herself and herself' (Gilbert and Gubar 1979: 17). In other words, since the literary tradition is taken to be primarily male, since Shakespeare's sister has to be invented or imagined, by Virginia Woolf, in the first place, female writers suffer from an 'anxiety of authorship', from a fundamental difficulty in defining and exploring and articulating their own identities. Women writers suffer from a 'radical fear' that they cannot create, a fear that 'the act of writing will isolate or destroy' them (p. 49). Gilbert and Gubar argue that such an anxiety is 'profoundly debilitating' to women as writers, even as it is, at the same time, the very topic of their writing, the very impetus of their authorship (p. 51).

Feminist literary criticism is of course far from a homogeneous discourse, and while critics like Elaine Showalter and Gilbert and Gubar were attempting to establish a female literary tradition, to configure the female author, other feminist critics and theorists were arguing in diametrically opposed ways against what they saw as Gilbert and Gubar's biological or social determinism. While critics such as Gilbert and Gubar have, as Mary Jacobus puts it, 'no option but to posit the woman author as origin and her life as the primary locus of meaning' (Jacobus 1986: 108), an alternative approach to feminist engagements with the 'death of the author' is to welcome that 'death', to argue, indeed, that for a true feminist criticism to flourish the very concept of the author, like the concept of the name, of identity, even of 'man' and 'woman', must be challenged, subverted or deconstructed. Thus, poststructuralist feminists argue that the idea of the author is itself a masculine or patriarchal 'construct' – that the 'authority' of the author is itself an intrinsic aspect of patriarchy. As Peggy Kamuf argues, the danger that critics such as Gilbert and Gubar face is that in describing a female tradition of authorship they simply repeat and reinforce patriarchal ways of knowing. Kamuf argues that patriarchy has always allowed a separate category for 'the intellectual or cultural productions of women', whereby women are construed as special or 'exceptional' and therefore marginal in a culture that reserves for masculinity the position of the universal. Moreover, for Kamuf, such critics reinforce the 'cult of the individual' and the insistence on literature as the 'expressions, simple and direct, of individual experience', concepts which are themselves part of the patriarchal thinking of authorship: in focusing on the exceptional individual, Kamuf argues, such critics confirm the 'patriarchal heritage' of the proper name, that 'mask' inherited from the father (Kamuf 1980: 286). And in *Sexual/Textual Politics* (1985), Toril Moi explicitly links patriarchy with authorship when she declares that the author is the 'source, origin and meaning of the text' for the patriarchal critic and that to 'undo this patriarchal practice of *authority*' feminist critics need to 'proclaim with Roland Barthes the death of the author' (Moi 1985: 62–3).

Poststructuralist feminism, particularly the *écriture féminine* theorized and practised by the French writers Luce Irigaray, Hélène Cixous and Julia Kristeva in the mid-1970s, asserts, therefore, 'not the sexuality of the text but the textuality of sex' (Jacobus 1986: 109). In this regard, poststructuralist feminism is concerned to avoid the trap of essentialism or biological determinism, the idea that there just is a universal 'essence' of woman, that she is 'naturally', biologically determined, seeing such determinations as fundamental to patriarchy's intellectual defence of the oppression of women. Rather than a natural or biological essence to femininity, the 'feminine role' involves mimicry: it must be assumed, deliberately (Irigaray 1985: 76). Woman 'must write her self', must 'put herself into the text' (Cixous 1997: 347). Or, in a rather different, more recent return to the question, women must be understood (like men) to enact or 'perform' gender identity (Butler 1990). There is a strong sense, in other words, that femininity is constructed or assumed, that the author is herself part of a performance of subjectivity, of subjectivity as gendered.

Theorists such as Irigaray and Cixous may be said, though, to be playing an impossible, a double, game, at once resisting the identity of femininity or female authorship and at the same time nevertheless trying to characterize it, attempting in particular to identify it with a certain mode of writing (with feminine writing or *écriture féminine*), a mode of writing that is characterized precisely in opposition to masculinity. While on the one hand 'woman' can only be identified through her lack of identity, as 'this sex which is not one', in Irigaray's phrase, on the other hand this very absence of identity itself constitutes an identity. 'Woman must put her self into the text', then, in Cixous's memorable declaration, 'woman must write woman', even though it remains 'impossible to *define* a feminine practice of writing' (Cixous 1997: 347, 348, 353). The impossibility of defining women's writing, in other words, doesn't prevent Cixous and Irigaray from doing so. And, more worryingly, despite claims that *écriture féminine* can be performed or produced by men and women (or that it is a discourse in which such terms are displaced or questioned or deconstructed) it nevertheless turns out to be constituted as a way of writing that in fact takes its direction precisely from patriarchal stereotypes of 'femininity'. The title essay from Irigaray's book *This Sex Which is Not One* (1977) is particularly clear in this respect:

> 'She' is indefinitely other in herself. This is doubtless why she is said to be whimsical, incomprehensible, agitated, capricious . . . not to mention her language, in which 'she' sets off in all directions leaving 'him' unable to discern the coherence of any meaning. Hers are contradictory words, somewhat mad from the standpoint of reason, inaudible for whoever listens to them with ready-made grids, with a fully elaborated code in hand. For in what she says, too, at least when she dares, woman is constantly touching herself. She steps ever so slightly aside from herself with a murmur, an exclamation, a whisper, a sentence left unfinished. . . . When she returns, it is to set off again from elsewhere. From another point of pleasure, or of pain. One would have to listen with another ear, as if hearing an 'other meaning' always in the process of weaving itself, of embracing itself with words, but also of getting rid of words in order not to become fixed, congealed in them. For if 'she' says something, it is not, it is already no longer, identical with what she means. What she says is never identical with anything, moreover; rather it is contiguous. It touches upon.
>
> (Irigaray 1985: 29)

Despite the influence of the idea of *écriture féminine* and despite its important qualifications of the essentialism of other, more traditional forms of feminist criticism, it seemed to many to end up in an impasse –

an impasse of the attempt to describe what should, strictly speaking, be beyond definition and description. Irigaray's is a bold attempt to describe the indefinable in women's authorship, but it too easily falls into the trap of expressing what it is designed to avoid, and it can too easily be read as an essentialist statement about a universal, biological femininity.

While feminist criticism is very far from limited to the two strands briefly outlined here, we might see from this brief discussion that authorship, authorial identity, is an important element in these projects. From the retrieval of a female tradition, interventions in canon-formation, and studies of the social and cultural conditions of women writers, to attempts to define an oppositional feminine identity and mode of writing, feminisms are necessarily bound up with the theory of authorship and indeed themselves constitute theories of authors.

NEW HISTORICISM

As we have seen in Chapter 2, above, discussions of the social history of authorship, especially of the emergence of authorship in its modern form in the seventeenth and eighteenth centuries, have been particularly prominent in literary studies in the last two decades, and many of these studies share features of so-called new historicist criticism. New historicism, a strand of historical criticism influenced by certain forms of poststructuralism, particularly the work of Michel Foucault, involves a 'return to history' in which history is understood to be textual, to be recorded and interpreted, but also to be structured and even constructed in and through texts. The point is made most succinctly in Louis Montrose's famous slogan from an essay on the principles of new historicism, 'Professing the Renaissance' (1989): 'the historicity of texts and the textuality of history' (Montrose 1998: 781). In this section, I want to suggest that, alongside the interest that new historicists have shown in developing Foucault's ideas about the history of the author, this return to history, this turn to a textualized historicism, is itself more generally bound up with the question of the author. I want to suggest that since new historicists are concerned with the modes of production of literary texts, they inevitably come up against questions of authorship. Indeed, the new historicism or 'cultural poetics' espoused by Montrose, Stephen Greenblatt and others seems to involve a certain ambivalence with regard to the question of subjectivity

– or to the 'subjectivity effect', as Joel Fineman calls it (Fineman 1991) – around which any concern with the author will necessarily revolve. As Jean E. Howard notes, while there is for Greenblatt in particular a concern for 'a provisional and contradictory self which is the product of discourse' in new historicism there is at the same time 'a lingering nostalgia' for 'individual lives' (Howard 1986: 37).

It is possible, then, to understand new historicism as revolving around precisely the question of authorship, around authorial identity, based as it is on an often highly sophisticated analysis of the kinds of cultural and political forces by which individual authors are constituted and in relation to which they write. In new historicism, the author's consciousness, his or her subjectivity or intention, even his or her life, are reconceived as historical and textual, subject to and the subject of the discursive dynamics of the circulations of power. One of the characteristic gestures of Greenblatt's work, for example, is to link a canonical English text with a colonial practice, discourse, signifying system, or event of which the author of the canonical work was not, could not have been, aware. And, as Catherine Gallagher and Stephen Greenblatt remark, in looking at different, distant cultures, they are looking for 'something that the authors we study would not have had sufficient distance upon themselves and their own era to grasp' (Gallagher and Greenblatt 2000: 8). Nevertheless, the author may still be shown to stand at the still centre of the literary text in new historicist readings. Montrose, for example, explains that the focus of new historicism is on the 'refiguring of the socio-cultural field within which . . . literary and dramatic works were originally produced' (Montrose 1998: 779). While new historicism resists the traditional 'privileging' of the 'unified and autonomous individual' of the Author, or even in fact, as Montrose says, of the Work (p. 780), the fact that it is concerned with the 'original' scene of production allows for the question of authorship, albeit within a newly conceived 'socio-cultural field'. New historicism rejects the 'romantic' ascription of agency to the isolated, autonomous author, since it is concerned with the 'social production of "literature"'. But it is also nevertheless concerned with what Montrose refers to as the constructed 'subjectivities of social beings' (p. 782). The distinction between the subjectivities of autonomous individuals and the subjectivities of social beings is important because of the particular ways in which authors, texts, and historical events are reconceived in new historicism. But the approach still focuses on authors, authors as 'social beings', in its analysis of texts and history. Greenblatt makes this clear in his essay 'Resonance and Wonder', one of the most well-known and most clarifying statements of his intellectual position. While new historicism 'eschews' universalist ideas of 'man', he explains, it nevertheless insists on individual agency, agency based around 'selves' that are 'fashioned and acting according to the generative rules and conflicts of a given culture':

> Actions that appear to be single are disclosed as multiple; the apparently isolated power of the individual genius turns out to be bound up with collective, social energy; a gesture of dissent may be an element in a larger legitimation process, while an attempt to stabilize the order of things may turn out to subvert it.
>
> (Greenblatt 1990: 164–5)

The figure of a newly socialized author remains prominent in such descriptions of new historicism's project: the phenomenon of the individual 'genius' is not denied, the 'gesture of dissent' still a gesture, and if single actions are 'disclosed as multiple', this doesn't eliminate an individual's participation in that collective process.

The investment of new historicism in a traditional sense of authorship is most clearly revealed in the context of its engagement with the work of William Shakespeare. To put it simply, new historicism needs to account for the extent to which Shakespeare is seen, by new historicists as much as by others, as exceptional. In 'Invisible Bullets', for example, Stephen Greenblatt argues that Shakespeare's concern with 'the production and containment of subversion and disorder' is part of a more general concern amongst those involved in the Elizabethan theatre to exploit 'some of the fundamental energies of . . . political authority'. But in a crucial concession, he suggests that Shakespeare 'contrived to absorb more of these energies into his plays than any of his fellow playwrights':

> He succeeded in doing so because he seems to have understood very early in his career that power consisted not only in dazzling display . . . but also in a systematic structure of relations. . . . Shakespeare evidently grasped such strategies not by brooding on the impact of English culture on far-off Virginia but by looking intently at the world

immediately around him, by contemplating the queen and her powerful friends and enemies, and by reading imaginatively the great English chroniclers.

(Greenblatt 1988: 39–40)

As much as any old-fashioned biographical critic and as much as any besotted Romantic poet, in this essay Greenblatt privileges Shakespeare and imagines what he saw, how he understood, what he thought and what he 'brooded' upon. The difference is that for Greenblatt what Shakespeare thinks, contemplates, sees and broods upon are the cultural 'energies' of a particular society. Shakespeare's mind, in other words, is imagined as full of the social, imagined as being constructed in and by the society in which he lived. But it is still Shakespeare's mind, his individuality, his consciousness, that accounts for the exceptionality of his work. In fact, Greenblatt's essay characteristically moves from author to text to the Elizabethan stage to Elizabethan society and back again in a series of moves that may be said to characterize new historicist configurations of socialized authorship. Thus, in just a couple of paragraphs Greenblatt moves from a statement about the play's self-consciousness (*Henry V* is 'remarkably self-conscious'), to an assertion about Shakespeare's awareness (the poet is 'intensely aware'), and a statement about Shakespeare's projection of his professional self onto his hero (there is an 'underlying complicity' in the Henriad between the prince and the playwright), to a wider sense of Elizabethan culture (to understand this complicity we need a 'poetics of Elizabethan power'), and finally to the specific arena of the Elizabethan stage (such a 'poetics of Elizabethan power' is 'inseparable . . . from a poetics of the theater') (pp. 63–4).

Greenblatt's authorialism involves, in the end, something like a nostalgic desire for a lost author, just as there is often a plangent sense of his own authorship, an almost melancholy yearning for an other, younger self understood as part of a cultural and familial inheritance in his work. 'I want to bear witness', Greenblatt remarks at the end of his ground-breaking book *Renaissance Self-Fashioning*, 'to my overwhelming need to sustain the illusion that I am the principle maker of my own identity' (Greenblatt 1980: 257). 'I began with the desire to speak with the dead', he begins his next book, *Shakespearean Negotiations* (Greenblatt 1988: 1). 'I wanted to know where [Shakespeare] got the matter he was working with and what he did with that matter', he comments most recently in *Hamlet in Purgatory* (Greenblatt 2001: 4; see also 5–9). The author in new historicism is, then, a central, organizing presence, even as it is conceived of as a textual effect and as submerged within or embraced by the circulation of social and political energies and the discourses and structures of power. New historicism, we might conclude, is another way of conceiving of the author, or, more properly perhaps, a way of conceiving the author as other. New historicism is, in the end, formed around and internally divided by a certain configuration of authorship.

5

COLLABORATION

The collaborator is one who works with another, a co-labourer. Aside from the sense of the traitor, one who works with the enemy, a sense originating in the Second World War, the word is primarily used about authors. The surprisingly sparse entry in the *OED* for 'collaborator' identifies its first use in 1802, suggesting that collaboration becomes significant, comes to signify, within an ideology of authorship as singular, individual, unique, within the context of the rise of what Jack Stillinger calls the Romantic 'myth of the solitary genius'. The idea of literary collaboration, in other words, seems only to have become a matter for consideration, seems only to need its own word, once the Romantic conception of authorship, with its emphasis on expression, originality and autonomy, emerges as the dominant 'ideology' of composition. Collaboration, in this narrative, disrupts the regal isolation, the solitary individualism, of the Romantic author and is conceived of as an aberration or a marginal literary mode. In this chapter, I begin by looking at the varieties of collaboration and ask whether it may, rather, be seen as normative, as the normal mode of literary production, against which individual authorship should itself be measured. I then go on to look at that most collaborative of cultural forms, film. One of the most significant developments in film theory in the twentieth century was the *auteurist* movement, an approach to the cinema that, in an arguably perverse, counter-factual gesture of authorialism, privileges the singular, originating author-figure of the director.

MULTIPLE AUTHORSHIP

Well-known examples of conventional literary collaborations include the plays of Shakespeare, several of which involved significant elements of collaboration; the fifteen co-written plays of Francis Beaumont and John Fletcher (including *Philaster* (1609) and *The Maid's Tragedy* (1610–11)); Joseph Addison and Richard Steele's *The Spectator* (1711–12); the *Lyrical Ballads* of William Wordsworth and Samuel Taylor Coleridge (1798); two novels by Joseph Conrad and Ford Madox Ford (*The Inheritors* (1900) and *Romance* (1903)); T.S. Eliot's *The Waste Land* (1922), a poem drastically cut, edited, shaped and revised by Ezra Pound; and the multi-lingual *Renga* (1969) by Octavio Paz, Charles Tomlinson, Jacques Berthoud and Edoardo Sanguineti. But such collaborations are often seen as exceptions that prove the rule of solitary authorship. In certain forms of post-Romantic criticism, collaboration even in this limited sense has the whiff of scandal, indeed, and is seen as something like literature's shameful family secret, a shared vice of writing. The significance of collaboration has therefore often been elided or even denied: either the *extent* of the collaboration in a particular text is downplayed or it is argued that the aesthetic *value* of the collaborative work is compromised by its dissipation within the mind of more than one creative agent. Literary criticism has developed a series of strategies to cope with these dissonant collaborations. Shakespeare's plays are scrutinized to distinguish the bard's words from the infection of other hands; Beaumont and Fletcher, contemporaries of Ben Jonson and William Shakespeare, are seen as minor writers in this company; Addison and Steele's *The Spectator* is said to be no more than a particularly exalted form of literary journalism; the collaboration of Wordsworth and Coleridge is understood to be limited to a few lines from 'The Rime of the Ancient Mariner', the opening stanza of 'We are Seven', a couple of minor poems, and the shared thinking of the 1800 Preface; the results of Conrad's collaboration with Ford are seen as among Conrad's weakest works; Pound's influence on *The Waste Land* is held to be no more than an editorial intrusion since, after all, T.S. Eliot's *The Waste Land* is not T.S. Eliot and Ezra Pound's *The Waste Land*; and because of its multiple authorship *Renga* is, according to one critic writing in the mid-1990s, 'yet to receive its due' (Clark 1997: 222). 'Occasionally, for sport and in despair', comments William Gass, sceptical of *Renga* and other collaborations, 'fiction writers will alternate the writing of a novel's chapters, and equally rarely, talents like Ford's and Conrad's will collaborate with a modest sort of success'. But in most cases, Gass declares, the efforts result in 'schoolboy botches' (Gass 1985: 272).

Nevertheless, critics have recently started to see collaboration as more than just an aberrant or marginal procedure. Indeed, critics have even begun to suggest that collaboration may be conceived as a *primary* mode of composition. In his study of collaboration and the 'myth of the solitary genius', for example, Jack Stillinger suggests that 'multiple authorship', far from being a freak of nature, an exception to the rule, is in fact a 'frequently occurring phenomenon' and that it has been, despite the romantic myth, 'one of the routine ways of producing literature all along' (Stillinger 1991: 201). Stillinger includes, as an Appendix to his book, a list of texts produced through the work of multiple authorship but not formally acknowledged as such on the title-page. He limits his list to the Romantic and post-Romantic periods, explaining that collaboration in earlier periods was so common as to make such a list self-defeating: his book in fact suggests that it might be easier to list texts which were *not* the product of collaboration in some form before the nineteenth century. Expanding the definition of collaboration to include various forms of co-writing, Stillinger lists, amongst others, John Cam Hobhouse's footnotes to Byron's *Childe Harold*, Canto 4; Mary Shelley's editing of Percy Bysshe Shelley's posthumous poems, and his 'help' in her *Frankenstein*; the publisher John Taylor's 'extensive editing' of John Clare's poems; Henry Adams's 'use of his wife's letters' in *Democracy* and *Esther*; the editorial alterations to Hardy's serialized novels; the 'editorial rewriting' of Emily Dickinson's poems; the presence of 'other hands' in Oscar Wilde's *The Importance of Being Earnest*; Ford Madox Ford and Edward Garnett's contributions to Conrad's *Nostromo*; the publisher's censorship of James Joyce's *Dubliners*; Hugh MacDiarmid's plagiarism in 'A Drunk Man Looks at the Thistle' as well as Herman Melville's in *Moby Dick* and D.M. Thomas's in *The White Hotel*; the 'editorial creation' of Barbara Pym's posthumously published *An Academic Question* from two separate drafts; the 'significant changes' by their respective trade editors of Dashiel Hammett's *Red Harvest*, E.E. Cummings's *The Enormous Room*, and John Dos Passos's *Three Soldiers*; F. Scott Fitzgerald's 'influence' on Hemingway's *The Sun Also Rises* and the 'influence of friends' on Robert Lowell's 'collective poetry'; the fact that James Michener's novels were partly written by a 'research team'; and Ted Hughes's posthumous arrangement of the poems in Sylvia Plath's *Ariel* (Stillinger 1991: 204–13). This limited selection from Stillinger's already highly selective list might suggest not only how often collaborative writing occurs in the literary canon, but the sheer variety of forms that such collaboration or 'multiple authorship' can take, from editorial intervention to legal or commercial censorship, from the appropriation of others' private letters to plagiarism, from unspecified 'help' to extensive editing.

But intriguing as it is, and challenging as it is to our sense that outside a limited number of well-documented collaborations composition involves the work of a solitary individual, Stillinger's list does not necessarily challenge conventional notions of authorship as fundamentally individual and solitary. Authors may rely on editors to correct their spelling and prepare their poems for publication (as in the case of John Clare), they may plagiarize other writers (as in the case of Melville and others), they may turn letters by friends and lovers into poetry (as in the case of Robert Lowell), but such procedures do not necessarily affect our sense that a text originates with an individual author. Despite Stillinger's suggestion that we should read texts differently in the light of such extensive and varied modes of collaboration, there is no great difficulty in accommodating such forms of collaboration to conventional understandings of autonomous literary production: John Clare's poems can be re-edited from manuscript and without editorial 'intrusion', or it can be understood that in some sense Clare *intended* the editorial revisions that Taylor supplies; once one has identified them, it is possible to bracket elements of plagiarism in Melville and others or even to read such literary 'kidnappings' (to use one of plagiarism's etymological senses) in terms of the plagiarizing author's intentions; and it is possible – and not uncommon, indeed – to admire the mastery with which Lowell turns the informality of a personal letter into the formal artwork of a poem. In much the same way, where critics come up against texts that have been co-authored, much energy is often put into establishing the origin of individual parts of the work. In this sense too, collaborative authorship needn't challenge the conception of the author as single and autonomous. Thus, for example, there is a whole section of the Shakespeare industry devoted to the identification of what is authentically Shakespearean in works that involve other 'hands'. In the early twentieth century, the critic J.M. Robertson devised a neat solution to the problem by attributing anything in a Shakespeare play that might compromise the bard's 'superhumanly high standards' to other writers who have 'tampered' with his work (Vickers 2002a: 137). Another, usually amateur, part of the industry is devoted to proving that Shakespeare did not in fact write Shakespeare's plays at all, and that they were written by Sir Francis Bacon, Christopher Marlowe, Edward De Vere, William Stanley, Roger Manners or even Queen Elizabeth I. Indeed, in what only appears to be a paradox, the whole quasi-scientific discipline of attribution studies is devoted to a fundamental belief in both the intricate collaborations of literary production and the integrity of individual authorship (see for example Foster 2001, Love 2002, Vickers 2002a and 2002b): as Harold Love comments, 'The subject of attribution studies is the uniqueness of each human being and how this is enacted in writing' (Love 2002: 4). The work of attributionists is based on a fundamental concern for the integrity of the individual signature, for indelible signs or traces of authorial identities that, they believe, remain in the work.

In *Attributing Authorship* (2002), Harold Love is able to argue that 'most historical acts of writing' are in fact collaborative by enlarging the category of collaboration to include aspects of literary production usually overlooked in this context (Love 2002: 220). As Love points out, the 'Romantic' model of authorship as the work of a single, autonomous individual overlooks 'all that precedes the act of writing (language acquisition, education, experiences, conversation, reading of other authors)' as well as everything that comes after the initial act of inscription, as the work is 'vetted by friends and advisers, receives second thoughts and improvements, is edited for the press . . . and given the material form in which it will encounter its readers' (p. 33). Love usefully distinguishes a number of different types of collaborative authorship, a set of 'linked activities' or '*authemes*' as he calls them (p. 39). 'Precursory authorship' designates the way in which a prior text can be the source for or an influence on a later one. This category includes, for example, the incorporation of others' arguments, narratives, scenes, phrases or words into a text, as in the case of Shakespeare's use of historical sources, appropriations that, for the Middle Ages and the Renaissance, constituted a proper deference to authority. 'Executive authorship' is Love's term for the situation in which two or more individuals collaborate to devise and order a text or a series of texts: Addison and Steele's *The Spectator* is a famous example from the early eighteenth century, but even more familiar is the anonymous 'editorial' that remains a feature of many newspapers. 'Declarative authorship' involves an individual *validating* a work for which she provides little or none of the actual material: the case of the politician whose speeches are scripted by aides or that of the film star whose autobiography is 'ghosted' by a professional writer are familiar examples. Finally, Love's category of 'revisionary authorship' includes the work of publishers' editors in 'polishing' a novel or, more visibly, such arrangements as John Middleton Murry's posthumous editing of Katherine Mansfield's journals or Ezra Pound's revisions to T.S. Eliot's *The Waste Land* (Love 2002: 39–50).

Love's analysis of these four forms of collaboration usefully organizes the varied examples presented by Jack Stillinger. But since Love is concerned with the question of attribution, his interest in studying collaboration is, finally, to establish the distinction between one individual's authorship and another's. As I have suggested, the logic of attribution studies is rather to confirm than to question or disturb the notion of the individuality and autonomy of the author. But a similar logic can even be said to be at work in studies designed to disrupt, by historicizing, conventional notions of autonomous authorship. In *Milton, Authorship, and the Book Trade* (1999), for example, Stephen Dobranski addresses the question of early modern authorship and attempts to establish the importance of the culture of collaboration in the seventeenth century in a study that also finally confirms the individuality of authorship. Dobranski points out that whereas the early eighteenth-century book trade began ruthlessly to exploit the power of the author's name to increase the market for literary works, most printed material in the mid- to late seventeenth century was by contrast published anonymously (Dobranski 1999: 18). In the seventeenth-century book trade, Dobranski argues, the process of publishing a book was itself commonly seen as collaborative, and authority for the book 'was dispersed among several people, each of whom to a varying degree could influence its form, profit from its publication, and be held accountable for its contents to others' (p. 26). He suggests that Milton's construction of his own authorship as solitary and individual was produced, paradoxically, through a process of collaboration with 'amanuenses, acquaintances, printers, distributors, and retailers' (p. 9). Dobranski argues that literary critics have applied the 'principle of unity' from an anachronistic logic of authorship in order to explain any contradictions and inconsistencies in Milton's work. But he suggests that such inconsistencies should instead be seen as allowing us a 'glimpse' beyond the 'theoretical construction' of the author to the 'real person, John Milton, operating within his specific historical environment' (p. 133). 'Rather than positing a coherent set of beliefs for Milton', Dobranski suggests, 'we need to understand his various literary acts as products of the changing communities in which he participated' (p. 182).

Nevertheless, Dobranski's book is in fact structured around the idea of the Romantic author-figure even as it attempts to explore the *differences* from the Romantic myth of solitary genius in Milton's practice. As Dobranski himself acknowledges, this is evinced by the fact that his study is based unequivocally around the singular figure of John Milton (p. 182). It is through Milton that everything must pass before emerging as *Samson Agonistes, Paradise Lost* or *Areopagitica,* and the many and varied contributors to these texts – the publishers, printers, booksellers, editors, censors, that Dobranski discusses – seem, in the end, only to confirm the controlling presence of the poet. The kind of dispersal and multiplication of authorship that is proposed in Dobranski's study in fact evinces a manifestation of the author-figure in terms of what Roger Chartier, following Foucault, refers to as the author's 'primordial function of guaranteeing the unity and the coherence of the discourse' (Chartier 1994: 46). Thus, Dobranski's suggestion that we can explain the tensions within Milton's work by examining the contradictory commercial and political pressures under which the poet was working may be understood as a way of asserting the 'unity' of Milton's authorship. As with other studies of collaboration, Dobranski's apparently revisionary study of Milton's collaborative authorship in fact finally returns us to a traditional conception of the author as singular, as an originating individual, and to criticism as the evaluation of what Dobranski calls the poet's 'true face' (p. 183).

Much recent debate around authorship, particularly with respect to literary collaboration, has similarly focused on the early modern period, the period before the Romantic ideology allegedly took hold of the institution of literature and the cultural construction of authorship, before the individual author's ownership of his or her work becomes enforceable in law. This, it is claimed, was a time when the ideology of possessive individualism was emergent, contested and yet to be securely embedded within its economic, cultural and political formations. The early modern theatre in particular is understood to be a site of multiple, and often undeclared, collaborations in which authorship is often erased or indiscernible; playbills, for example, only began to ascribe works to individual authors at the end of the seventeenth century. In a powerful if controversial study of this topic in the context of the early modern stage, *Textual Intercourse: Collaboration, Authorship, and Sexualities in Renaissance Drama* (1997), Jeffrey Masten goes rather further than Dobranski in analysing the dislocating and disseminating effects of collaboration. Masten argues that collaboration was the 'dominant mode of production' in the sixteenth- and seventeenth-century theatre, and proposes that we revise our sense that multiple authorship is 'an aberrant form of textual production' accordingly: we should, Masten proposes, 'forego anachronistic attempts to divine the singular author of each scene, phrase, and word' (Masten 1997: 14, 7). Masten's book is directed towards a reconsideration of Shakespeare's authorship since, as 'the very anti-type of collaboration', Shakespeare has commonly been seen as '*the* individual Author and the author of individuality' (p. 10) despite the prevalence of collaboration in early modern drama generally and the fact that Shakespeare was known to have collaborated on a number of works (some of which are usually ascribed to his sole authorship). Masten argues that texts that have survived from this period are often those that have been revised either by the first author(s) or by others for a later revival; that actors, directors, copyists and others regularly rearranged, cut, and augmented texts; that censorship was itself an active element in many a play's 'final' or acted form; that dramatists were also invariably actors in a company, rather than having a separate authorial role; and that in fact theatrical collaboration in the Renaissance 'was predicated on *erasing* the perception of any differences that might have existed' between the work of the play's various authors (p. 17). Instead of seeing collaboration as a 'more *multiple* version of authorship', a 'doubling' of 'author/ity', Masten insists, it should instead be seen as involving a 'dispersal' of authorship and of the authority that it assumes (p. 19). We should, he argues, see texts and indeed language itself as a social 'process of exchange', as part of the circulation of 'homosocial' or 'homoerotic' energies, indeed, rather than as the product of an individual: 'rather than policing discourse off into agents, origins, and intentions, a collaborative focus elaborates the social mechanism of language, discourse as intercourse', Masten declares (p. 20). For Renaissance drama, at least, the convention of interpreting texts in terms of the intentions, the biography, or the personality of a unique individual is, if Masten is right, wildly inappropriate, if also, as the existence of his book itself suggests, extraordinarily tenacious.

Masten's study has recently been the subject of at least one vigorous critique and it is worth briefly looking at the counter-arguments to his conception of Renaissance authorship. In the Appendix to his recent study of Shakespearean collaboration, *Shakespeare, Co-Author* (2002), Brian Vickers launches a stringent attack on Masten's book, arguing against what he sees as the theory-driven incoherence and historical inaccuracy of Masten's Foucauldian argument: 'Every point in [Foucault's] history of the "late emergence of the author" is dubious', Vickers asserts, 'if not obviously wrong' (Vickers 2002a: 509). While not denying the importance of collaboration in the early modern theatre, Vickers defends 'authorship studies' (the computer-aided stylometric analysis of authorial attribution) against Masten's argument that identifying individual authorial style in the context of the sixteenth and seventeenth centuries is itself an anachronistic imposition of post-Romantic conceptions of subjectivity and authorship. When Masten argues that the ascription of texts to individual authors is 'anachronistic' in the context of the early modern period, Vickers counter-charges that Masten's own book is historically 'amnesiac' (p. 540), that it is itself anachronistic with regard to the actual and historically verifiable practices of the Elizabethan, Jacobean and Caroline stage, of what Vickers calls the historical 'figures of flesh and blood busily earning their living by their pens' (p. 539). In the 'Elizabethan theatre world', Vickers declares, 'the author had not just "emerged", he had established himself as an independent agent, intellectually and economically' (p. 540).

Attribution studies as it is practised and defended by Vickers involves, then, a fundamental belief that 'writers have distinct and individual styles' and that these styles are expressed both on the 'conscious level' in terms of the shaping and ordering of a work and its rhetoric, and through the 'unconscious' adoption of verbal mannerisms. Attribution studies proposes that as long as we have access to other works by the individuals concerned, these authorial or stylistic signatures can be unequivocally discriminated (p. 506). It is possible of course largely to separate the individual contributions of Pound from those of Eliot in *The Waste Land* because we have the manuscripts to prove it. But Vickers and other attributionists propose that even without such evidence, linguistic style alone leaves verifiable traces of the authorship of individual scenes, passages, sentences in collaborative works.

The debate between Masten and Vickers involves disagreements over questions of historical verification, empirical evidence, and early modern procedures for the composition of dramatic texts. On another level, though, the debate involves even more fundamental concerns over conceptions of individuality and subjectivity and over the very nature of personhood and ultimately of authorship. In the end, the debate comes down to a fundamental difference between a conception of collaboration that maintains the distinction between individuals within a collaborative culture, and a 'poststructuralist' conception that suggests that individuality itself is split, divided, disseminated or dispersed within a literary culture that is radically multiple, fundamentally collaborative.

SINGULAR AUTHORSHIP: THE *AUTEUR*

Another context in which collaborative authorship may be said to complicate and even subvert Romantic notions of individual authorship is that of film. As Jack Stillinger has commented, the multiple agencies involved in the making of a film are normally so diverse and the process so intricately organized around a multitude of specialist trades and professions that 'for all practical purposes' authorship remains 'unassignable' (Stillinger 1991: 174). The person that writes the film script is conventionally seen as a minor player in the hierarchy of film production. More importance is often accorded the director, the actors, the cinematographer, the producer, the art director, the special effects or set designer, the software production team or the animator. But this multiplicity of authorizing agents itself produces particular problems for film critics. The upstart cultural discourse of film was, from the beginning, faced with the question of its cultural prestige. As Marjut Salokannel puts it, film contradicted the central tenets of the Romantic definition of art, art as authentic and irreproducible, as the 'unique creation of an individual author' and as the 'expression of genius' (Salokannel 2003: 154). In a procedure that might be seen to repeat an ancient strategy of cultural validation, film needed to find an author-figure in order to be recognized as an art form.

The problem of the author, of the apparent absence of the individual author in film, was addressed most directly in the so-called '*auteurist*' strand of French film theory that developed from the 1950s onwards. Although the use of the word *auteur* to talk about a film's director goes back as far as Jean Epstein's usage in 1921, it was in the late 1940s and 1950s that Jean-Luc Godard, Jacques Rivette, Eric Rohmer, François Truffaut and others writing in *Cahiers du Cinéma* first formulated the principles of *auteurism*. The aim of these writers and directors was 'to elevate the films of a few directors to the status of high art', as Virginia Wexman puts it, and to do so at the expense of what André Bazin called 'the genius of the system' (Wexman 2003: 3, 14). With such seminal essays as François Truffaut's 'A Certain Tendency in the French Cinema' (1954) and André Bazin's 'On the *Politique des auteurs*' (1957), the 'theory' of the *auteur*, theory that was in fact often no more than an assertion or gesture, a policy or attitude (Caughie 1981: 13), came to dominate academic film studies and more generally the discourse of cinema. Truffaut argued that French cinema should move away from the prevailing model of the 1950s, in which film was seen as subordinate to an original 'literary' text. Instead, he suggested, critics should develop an understanding and appreciation of the autonomous work and artistry of the filmmaker, focusing on the director's handling of the so-called *mise-en-scène*, the film's 'overall style', a style which included the acting, cutting, camera movement, distance and angle, and even the set and scenery (Wexman 2003: 3).

The privileging of the director as a film's 'author' involved a conscious resistance to the industrial film production of 1940s and 1950s Hollywood, a resistance to what Thomas Schatz calls the 'dehumanizing, formulaic, profit-hungry machinery of Hollywood's studio-factories'. As Schatz points out, *auteurism* involved a romanticized celebration of a small number of Hollywood directors (including John Ford, Alfred Hitchcock, Howard Hawks) whose 'personal style emerged' precisely through 'a certain antagonism toward the studio system at large' (Schatz 2003: 91).

The director, indeed, was only thought to be 'worth bothering with', as Andrew Sarris puts it, if he was capable of 'a sublimity of expression almost miraculously extracted' from the 'money-oriented environment' of the Hollywood studio (quoted in Schatz 2003: 91). The point was made very clearly in an early polemical essay on the artistry of film by the French critic Alexandre Astruc. Writing in 1948, Astruc argued that the 'caméra-stylo' or 'camera-pen' should be recognized as equivalent to the author's pen. Once that recognition has occurred, he suggested, cinema will have its author and would be afforded its proper place amongst the arts:

> The cinema is quite simply becoming a means of expression, just as all the arts have been before it, and in particular painting and the novel. After having been successfully a fairground attraction, an amusement analagous to boulevard theatre, or a means of preserving the images of an era, it is gradually becoming a language. By language, I mean a form in which and by which an artist can express his thoughts, however abstract they may be, or translate his obsessions exactly as he does in the contemporary essay or novel.
>
> (quoted in Caughie 1981: 9)

More nakedly than anywhere else, perhaps, Astruc exposes the linking of authorship with the question of 'cultural capital' that has always haunted author theory, and allows us to recognize that the question of authorship is inextricably bound up with the question of cultural prestige.

As *auteur* theory developed and became more sophisticated, the work of film criticism came to involve the detection of an underlying thematics of 'authorship', to involve the analysis of concealed traces of authorial expression, even of the expression of an authorial unconscious quite separate from intention itself. In the 1960s, for example, Fereydon Hoveyda's 'auteur-structuralism' developed a Lacanian form of film analysis in which the subject is hidden, marked only by discursive or filmic 'gaps', but in which 'the truth' of the subject can be revealed to the informed analyst. Hoveyda argued that the 'unconscious' of the *auteur* 'is written somewhere other than in the "apparent" chain of the images: in that which we call the "technique" of the *auteur*, in the choice of actors, in the decor and the relationship of the actors and objects with this decor, in the gestures, in the dialogue, etc' (quoted in Caughie 1981: 46–7). The

project of the film analyst therefore concerns the revelation of authorship, the presentation of the troubled subjectivity of the *auteur*-director,
within the filmic image. Such a strategy culminated in the kind of criticism
that Peter Wollen attempted in his 1972 book *Signs and Meanings in
the Cinema*. Here, Wollen attempted to align a highly romanticized,
idealized and indeed counter-factual construction of a filmic author with
a structuralist *critique* of authorial subjectivity. He attempted to discriminate his idea of film authorship from the Hollywood 'cult of personality',
suggesting that the director should not be seen as an 'individual' who
'express[es] himself or his own vision in the film' but should instead be
seen as a subject whose 'preoccupations' allow for 'unconscious, unintended meaning' to be 'decoded in the film, usually to the surprise of the
individual involved'. Auteur analysis, therefore, was seen to involve a
'tracing of a structure (not a message) within the work, which can then
post-factum be assigned to an individual, the director, on empirical
grounds' (Wollen 1981: 146).

The question of the author, then, has been central to the development
of film studies since the 1950s and the ascription of a single, unified and
identifiable author for a film or for a body of films is bound up with
the question of the status of film itself as a medium. To put it simply,
while film emerged in the early twentieth century as a commercial and
collaborative medium, in order to be taken seriously as an art, alongside
literature and the visual arts, it needed its own version of the myth of the
solitary genius (see Inge 2001: 628). Film needed to be redefined in terms
of the expression of the vision of a coherent and unified individual,
in terms of what the auteurist critic Andrew Sarris, writing in 1968, called
the 'doctrine of directorial continuity' (quoted in Wollen 2003: 76).
Indeed, Timothy Corrigan argues that auteurism may be seen in terms of
the industry's need 'to generate an artistic (and specifically Romantic)
aura, at a time when it was in danger of being overtaken by the new mass
media of TV' (Corrigan 2003: 96–7). What was needed was an 'organic,
controlling personality' arising, as it was thought to do for the Romantic
author, out of a 'troubled, biographical person' (Staiger 2003: 43).
As Colin MacCabe points out, however, the invention of the *auteur*
involved 'one massive contradiction': while theoretical work in linguistics,
psychoanalysis and Marxism was emphasizing the social construction of subjectivity, auteur-theory relied on a conception of individual

consciousness and agency that directly contradicted such discourses (MacCabe 2003: 40). The procedure seems of course particularly perverse in the context of a medium that rarely if ever involves the work of just one individual. Indeed, some would argue that rather than imposing a 'literary' model of authorship on film we should reconceive the apparently singular authorship of the literary text as itself cinematically collaborative: 'we need to recognise', Love suggests, that most novels are 'much more like films than we are prepared to acknowledge' and that, like films, they often deserve 'a long roll-call of credits at the end' (Love 2002: 37).

By its very nature, filmmaking is, as John Caughie puts it, 'a collective, commercial, industrial and popular' medium (Caughie 1981: 13). In retrospect, the whole project of *auteur* theory and *auterist* film analysis, like the sub-discipline of attribution studies, suggests above all the seemingly ineluctable cultural desire for the author. The counter-intuitive and counter-factual project of discerning an individual subjectivity at work as the ordering agent for the indisputably collaborative medium of film indicates the extent to which notions of 'art' and the cultural prestige on which it is based are bound up with a need for and an investment in a conception of the author as autonomous, unique, original and individual.

6

THE QUESTION OF LITERATURE

Writing in the Introduction to his collection of essays on *auteur* theory in 1981, John Caughie argued that 'the challenge to the concept of the author as source and centre of the text . . . has been decisive in contemporary criticism and aesthetic theory'. Late twentieth-century criticism and theory, Caughie proposed, are 'founded on that challenge, just as much of nineteenth- and twentieth-century philosophy was founded on the challenge to the centrality of God' (Caughie 1981: 1). But we might question just how decisive this challenge has been. Far from ridding the world of an authoritarian despot, the critique of authorship launched in the late 1960s by Barthes and Foucault may in fact be understood to have more securely fixed in place the question of the author in the interpretation of literary and other cultural texts.

Once you start looking for them, indeed, you find authors everywhere in contemporary literary culture. Writing in the middle of the eighteenth century, Samuel Johnson and Edward Young concurred in declaring *theirs* to be 'The age of Authors' (Johnson 1963: 457; Young 1918: 48), but the same could equally, or perhaps could more properly, be said of our own time. Contemporary culture seems to have an endless appetite for literary biographies, for example, or for newspaper and TV interviews with famous writers. Film adaptations of classic texts are 'branded' with the original author's name (*William Shakespeare's Romeo and Juliet* (1996), for example, or *Mary Shelley's 'Frankenstein'* (1994)), while university courses in literature are largely organized around the work of individual authors. And even postmodernism, with its alleged intolerance for the sentimental humanism, the comforting essentialism, of authorship, is nevertheless – or perhaps therefore – fascinated by, fixated on, author-effects and author-figures: one might think of Vladimir Nabokov's *Pale Fire* (1962), John Fowles's *The French Lieutenant's Woman* (1969), Gilbert Adair's *The Death of the Author* (1992), David Eggers's *A Heartbreaking Work of Staggering Genius* (2000), Salman Rushdie's *Fury* (2001), J.M. Coetzee's *Elizabeth Costello* (2003), or the stories of Jorge Luis Borges, Donald Barthelme and John Barth. Indeed, a major area of literary studies that we have hardly touched on in this book, the editing of literary texts, is fundamentally concerned with authorial intention. As D.D. Greetham comments, in spite of the influence of formalism, for most textual critics of the twentieth century intention was not a 'false question' but the 'primary' one (Greetham 1999: 161). James Thorpe, for example, declared that the editor's ideal is to 'present the text which the author intended'; G. Thomas Tanselle argued that the editor's task is to represent 'as closely as available evidence will allow, what the author wished his text to be'; and Fredson Bowers declared that the editor should attempt to recover 'the initial purity of an author's text' (quoted in Greetham 1999: 168).

In the first part of this chapter, I want to examine the pervasive presence of the author, of the 'institution' of authorship (Kamuf 1988), in the public face of the seemingly rather exclusive world of professional or academic literary criticism, and to suggest that authorship is central to the way in which critical practice is currently conceptualized and theorized within the wider public sphere of literary journalism and newspaper reviewing. I will then go on to look at a particular case, that of the reception of Ted Hughes's *Birthday Letters* (1998), in order to suggest that the centrality of authorship in contemporary culture has to do with the question of literature, with the question of what critics talk about when they talk about literature. In the third section of the chapter, I will develop this idea more generally in the context of literary theory and in relation to two propositions prompted in particular by the work of Jacques Derrida.

THE AUTHOR IN REVIEW

I want to begin with just three examples, arbitrarily selected from news-paper articles published in the week beginning 1 August 2003. The first is an essay in the London *Guardian* by the late Edward Said. The essay, by one of the preeminent Anglophone critics of the second half of the twentieth century, marks the twenty-fifth anniversary of the first publication of *Orientalism*, Said's ground-breaking examination of the construction of the orient in Western culture. As well as contemplating the reception of his book since its first publication, Said briefly describes his own literary-critical position as a 'humanist whose field is literature' (Said 2003: 5). He explains that his training as a comparative litera-ture specialist owes much to the great mid-twentieth-century European philologists Eric Auerbach, Leo Spitzer and Ernst Robert Curtius. In doing so, Said explicitly links his neo-philological approach to a certain sympathy for or identification with the author. 'The main requirement for the kind of philological understanding Auerbach and his predecessors were talking about and tried to practise', Said explains, 'was one that sympa-thetically and subjectively entered into the life of a written text as seen from the perspective of its time and its author.' Thus, Said continues, 'the interpreter's mind actively makes a place in it for a foreign "other"'. This making of a place for the alien other is, Said declares, 'the most important facet of the interpreter's mission' (p. 6). For Said, then, the task of the critic is to attend to this other, the author.

My second example is an essay by Barbara Everett in the *London Review of Books* on two recent publications, a selection from Samuel Taylor Coleridge's notebooks and a major scholarly edition of his poetry. Rather than commenting on her own critical practice, Everett makes a more general point about contemporary culture. 'This is an age of biography, not of poetry', Everett declares: an interest in 'daily existence' as exem-plified by the new edition of Coleridge's notebooks is preferred in 'the present moment in our culture', she suggests, to more 'élitist' questions provoked by 'formal literary arts' such as poetry (Everett 2003: 6). Everett goes on to suggest that what readers find interesting and attractive in poetry is in fact subordinated to this interest in biography, this interest in the author's life. Indeed, she links their fascination with biography to the question of canon formation. Those poems of Coleridge that have managed to capture readers' interest are memorable, she says, because of the way that they articulate 'what was real and disastrous in the poet's own life, both private and public' (p. 10). The success of Coleridge's three great dream-poems, 'Kubla Khan', 'The Ancient Mariner', and 'Christabel', their ability to 'lodge like an arrow in the creative memory', has to do with a paradoxical expression of personality within impersonality, a 'modernist' sense of impersonality which also includes the inscription of the writer's self within the poem. The self of the poet or artist is transformed into poetry or art. Through its influence on Sir Walter Scott, Everett argues, Coleridge's poetry had determining effects on the development of the English novel from the early nineteenth century onwards, an influence that has to do with the way that poems and novels can express 'the history of a culture' within 'the troubled experience of an individual' (p. 10). This authorcentric fascination is, acccording to Everett, fundamental to contemporary literary culture.

My third example from this journalistically fecund summer week is a lecture by Jonathan Bate given at a conference on 'The Condition of the Subject' organized by the English Subject Centre in London in July 2003 and published in edited form in the *Times Higher Education Supplement*, a weekly newspaper aimed at and read by the British academic community. Like Said and Everett, Bate foregrounds the role of the author in literary criticism. Bate laments the fact that for university students of English Literature in the twenty-first century there is 'so much theory to cover . . . that no room is left for some of the basics'. The 'basics' for Bate involves 'facts' and 'history', by which he means 'historical method', 'problems in biography' and the 'theory and practice of textual bibliography' (Bate 2003: 22). In fact, each of these sub-disciplines is intimately engaged with the question of authorship. Bate presents two examples. First, in the light of recent textual and statistical analysis of Shakespeare's *Titus Andronicus*, he suggests that we are now able to recognize that much of the play was in fact written by George Peele. As a consequence, Bate argues, there has been a shift in our perception of the play and indeed in our conception of Shakespeare's authorship, from the romanticized notion of the 'solitary genius' to a more fissiparous, if also more collective or collaborative, model of the 'team-player' (pp. 22–3). The second example concerns the poetry of John Clare. Bate explains that biographical research has revealed the extent to which the poet 'positively wanted his poems to be improved by his friends and editors' (p. 23), and he declares that, in the light of this knowledge, Clare's poetry should be both edited and read differently: the authentic Clare poem, the *authored* poem, should be understood to be produced in collaboration with the poet's publishers and friends. In both cases, Bate argues, a new, more accurate sense of the work results from a new and more accurate knowledge of the lives and writing methods of the two authors. Criticism, he suggests, is inextricably bound up with authorship.

Such instances of authorialism could be multiplied many times over in current literary journalism as well as in more specifically scholarly publications. Indeed, the institution of literary criticism, with its editions of authors' works, its literary biographies, its critical studies of individual authors, of influence, and of historical 'contexts', is inextricably engaged in studying questions of authorship. It is perhaps not too much to say that what we might call the recurring, seemingly interminable crisis of criticism (including 'crisis' in its etymological sense of crucial or deciding moment) itself turns on the question of authorship. Coming from different critical and theoretical perspectives, Said, Everett and Bate all suggest that questions of authorship are central to the critic's understanding of the proper task of criticism. And despite appearances, perhaps, these three critics are not *simply* reacting *against* poststructuralist or new-critical rejections of authorship. In fact, in each case I would suggest that the question of authorship itself continues to be a site of theoretical disturbance and concern. Each critic identifies authorship as the theoretical issue in their critical practice that must be explained and indeed defended: the problem of criticism, the problem of reading, *is* in the end the problem of authorship.

REVIEWING TED HUGHES'S *BIRTHDAY LETTERS*

In an interview published in the *Paris Review* in 1995, Ted Hughes spoke about the confessional impulse in poets: 'The real mystery is this strange need', he mused: 'Why do we have to blab? Why do human beings need to confess? Maybe, if you don't have that secret confession, you don't have a poem – don't even have a story. Don't have a writer' (quoted in Feinstein 2001: 229). The question of authorship and its troubled, troubling relationship to both critical practice and the very definition, the very institution of 'Literature', came into sharp focus with the publication of Ted Hughes's apparently 'confessional' collection of poems *Birthday Letters* in 1998. The reviews of this volume reveal in practice the crisis of criticism that I have referred to, and I want to suggest that the response to the volume in fact reflects a more general critical and theoretical concern with the question of the author in, and as, the question of literature.

Birthday Letters was Hughes's long-awaited response to the life, death, writing and critical reception of Sylvia Plath. Plath had taken her own life thirty-five years earlier, in the winter of 1963 after Ted Hughes had left her for another woman. Since her death, and not least as a result of the manner of her death, Plath's poetry had characteristically been read in terms of her life. And in the decades since her death, Hughes had regularly been blamed for the fact that Plath killed herself. After the publication of Plath's intimately revealing letters to her mother, *Letters Home* (1975), in particular, the sense that Hughes was in some way responsible for Plath's death had led to extraordinary scenes. On a poetry-reading tour of Australia, Hughes was met by demonstrators holding placards accusing him of murder; a poem making a similar accusation was published ('The Arraignment', by Robin Morgan (1972)); the name 'Hughes' was regularly obliterated from Plath's tombstone in Yorkshire; and Hughes was regularly denounced as a 'fascist' by protestors at public readings. Nevertheless, Hughes had rarely spoken publicly about his relationship with Plath, and the immediate critical and journalistic response to the publication of *Birthday Letters* therefore included fevered speculation about the possible biographical and autobiographical revelations that the volume might present. According to at least one critic, in fact, the reception of *Birthday Letters* 'proved' that 'gossip has displaced writing among the interests of many readers' (O'Brien 2003: 25). In this respect, the reviews of the volume constitute a uniquely clarifying instance of the way in which what M.M. Bakhtin calls the 'crisis of authorship' (Bakhtin 1990: 202–3) has become central to critical debate and interpretation. Just as Said, Everett and Bate place the question of authorship at the centre of their sense of literary-critical practice, each reviewer of *Birthday Letters* is led more-or-less explicitly to theorize authorship in order to justify his or her evaluation of Hughes's poetry. Each reviewer is impelled to judge the volume's literary value, to judge indeed its very *literariness*, in terms of a certain conception of authorship.

The publication of *Birthday Letters* in Britain was announced by the London *Times* in January 1998 with the publication of a selection of the poems. The poems were introduced by Hughes's successor as poet laureate, Andrew Motion. Motion immediately and unequivocally linked the selling of the poems, and the selling of the newspaper, to questions of biography and autobiography: the poems should be read, he suggested, for the insights that they offer the reader into not just one but two authors, not just Hughes but Plath too. And he introduced the volume, somewhat melodramatically, as 'a book written by someone obsessed, stricken and deeply loving': *Birthday Letters*, Motion suggested, allows us to reread other poems by Hughes, poems 'not specifically concerned with Plath', in terms of a man 'shaken into life by the earthquake shocks of her life and death'. What results, he declared, in a telling phrase, is of interest to 'everyone – professors as well as paparazzi' (Motion 1998: 22).

The central theoretical position, in Motion's short article and in the presentation and reception of *Birthday Letters* more generally, involves a subtle and often only implicit conception of the link between life and work. But like other commentators on the collection, Motion is troubled by this articulation. In a complex literary-critical manoeuvre, he suggests that the progress of the book enacts the progress of Plath's life but that this literary parallelism is also, paradoxically, an aestheticizing one: 'As the Ariel poems start to run', Motion declares, 'as Plath becomes increasingly volatile, and Hughes's need for self-protection intense, the language of the book becomes more symbolic and private'. The paradox allows the critic to escape the crude reductiveness of a biographical reading while also asserting the cogency of a certain biographicity: the 'great drive towards honesty' that Motion finds in Hughes's poems is also a form of secrecy. The more closely the poems are tied to biography, Motion argues, the more 'self-protective', the more 'symbolic and private' is the language of the poems. The more explicitly biographical they seem to become, then, the more private and more 'literary' they really are. While such poems are likely to be 'less admired' in the short term, Motion suggests, they will in 'the fullness of time' be considered the collection's 'finest achievement': they are, Motion declares, 'poetry staggering under the weight of its emotional load, but keeping its dignity and purpose'. In an assertion that fully articulates a certain millennial crisis of criticism, Motion explains that the reason why 'this book will live' has both to do with and not to do with its 'biographical value': 'Even if it were possible to set aside its biographical value (and why should we do that?), its linguistic, technical and imaginative feats would guarantee its future' (p. 22). Motion's rhetoric – his use of parentheses to ask the crucial, the biographical question, for example – exemplifies the contemporary anxiety of authorship and literary autobiography: why should we do that? why should we disallow a reading of the poem through the author and of the author through the poem? Simply to ask this question is to raise the possibility that we should in fact eschew such readings. Motion's concern with, and anxiety about, this question may be seen as a response to more than a century of intense debate over the role of authorship in literary criticism.

The crisis of authorship, then, itself defines both the journalistic presentation and the early critical response to Hughes's volume. And the crisis involves a fundamental questioning of the conception of poetry, and more generally of literature itself. It might seem odd that a book of poems, a book of eighty-eight short pieces of versified writing by one of the century's most significant poets, can be declared not to be poetry, but that is what is at stake in this crisis. So pervasive is this concern with the nature of authorship, with the status of the literary author, that the very question of what a poem *is*, the very definition of literature itself, is at stake in reviews of *Birthday Letters*. Thus, in at least two reviews of the volume there is a clear suggestion that just because they are so intimately tied to the life of the poet, Hughes's poems are not poems at all. Ian Hamilton is the most direct: 'But is it poetry?', he asks, at the end of a review in the London *Sunday Telegraph*. 'Well, not for me', he answers (Hamilton 1998: 7). *Birthday Letters* is instead a record of an affair, a record of a life and a death, and for that reason alone, not poetry, not literature. Precisely because of their biographical intimacy, precisely because of their authorialism, for Hamilton these poems are not poems. A similar point is made in a less direct way in a review by Edna Longley. 'Perhaps the most disturbing thing about *Birthday Letters* is Ted Hughes's lack of distance', Longley begins (Longley 1998: 27). The problem, she explains, is that the 'literary relationship between Hughes and Plath never separated the psychic from the poetic', a fact which she suggests entails a 'lack of poetic tact' (pp. 28, 27). Longley declares, somewhat primly, that the question of whether the volume constitutes poetry 'remains to be considered' (p. 28), eventually offering as a kind of answer to her question her wish that 'Hughes had written a memoir in the cool prose that sometimes tries to get out of his hectic poetry' (p. 30). It is poetry, in other words, but Longley wishes it wasn't. Frustrated by the undeservedly high praise that she feels Hughes has received for the volume, Longley laments the fact that Hughes's reputation is being 'talked up in some mysteriously collective way, and to hell with critical judgement, to hell with poetry' (p. 30).

Despite Longley's somewhat intemperate critique of what she calls the critical 'ravings' of the reviewers, others are often rather more circumspect, more qualified in their appraisals of the book's literary merits, and of its literariness. Many of them are nevertheless troubled by the book's (auto-)biographical aspect, sensing its biographicity as something to be explained or justified. Michael Glover, for example, makes the question of authorship and the definition of poetry or literature central to his concern with the volume. He suggests that the person, the personality, expressed by the poems is both profoundly distasteful and profoundly compelling. *Birthday Letters* is, he declares, 'ghoulish, obsessive and deeply engaging' (Glover 1998: 45). Hughes's attempt to 'unburden his psyche of all this terrible material' is 'ghoulish in the extreme, and as stagey as bad melodrama'. Poets, Glover insists, are 'generally secretive creatures' and a poem 'by its very nature, is a setting-apart, a raising up, and not some kind of versified anecdote' (p. 45). Like Andrew Motion, Glover resorts to the seemingly tautological reasoning that Hughes's poems are finally preserved from the impropriety and alleged unpoeticalness of autobiography by the sheer fact that they *are* indeed poems, by the fact that the more we read 'the more oblique and symbolic the poems become'. Poetry involves distance and disinterestedness, a separation from life, from the author, he suggests. For Glover, our *valuation* of poetry, indeed our very sense that it is poetry, depends on the disinterestedness of the literary speech act. Such questions are even more clearly addressed by Anthony Julius in *Poetry Review*. Julius suggests that Hughes had a 'double ambition': both to write about Plath '*and* to write poetry'. 'Are these negotiations successful?', Julius asks: 'Can the poems be read as anything other than interventions in the contest which is the history of Sylvia Plath?' (Julius 1998: 80). In response, he argues that we can never know the truth of Hughes's representation of his relationship with Plath and that we are therefore 'driven back to the poems as poetry'. 'There is always going to be this tension between the two voices', Julius remarks, 'a tension which poets reconcile in ways that are specific both to the truth of their love affair and to the truth of their art' (p. 81).

For Seamus Heaney, finally, the problem of autobiography in and as the problem of authorship is itself the problem of literature. In his review of Hughes's volume, Heaney argues that the poems have 'both an autobiographical and an archetypal resonance': they are about an individual and about the human condition. Nevertheless, like other critics Heaney is impelled to define the poems as poems in order to reassure us that they are indeed works of literature: 'The book's contents are unfailingly interesting', Heaney declares, but 'what makes *Birthday Letters* a poetic as opposed to just a publishing landmark is the valency of the poetry itself' (Heaney 1998: 11). Although they seem to have been written 'swiftly', as an immediate reaction to a memory of a life, Heaney argues, the poems also give the impression of 'utterance avalanching towards vision': 'suddenly the poem will take an extra jump, sure-footed and decisive, and land upon the thing that had been drawing it down from the memory path towards itself all along'. It is this effect of being 'drawn towards itself' that defines for Heaney the literariness of these poems. The poems evoke, in other words, not *just* a life, a past or history, but something more, something other, a 'sure-footed' leap, something beyond the self of the poet, something poetic, something that we can call poetry. But as a Nobel prize-winning poet as well as critic and reviewer, Heaney doesn't flinch from defining poetry as personal expression. For Ted Hughes, he argues, 'giving expression' to the trauma of Plath's death is 'more or less a genetic necessity': 'the work of poetry', Heaney concludes, 'is also necessarily a work of the purest self-absorption' (p. 11). Once again, Heaney is expressing the paradox, the crisis, that, as I have tried to suggest in Chapter 3, above, inhabits contemporary thinking about literature: the more personal a poem becomes the more it escapes personality.

In each case, then, and as is true more generally of the critical response to *Birthday Letters*, the reviewer confronts the question of authorship. And each time, the critic is forced to perform a series of critical-theoretical manoeuvres before arriving at a judgement of literary value. Poetry is first defined in terms of a certain relationship with, or detachment from, the poet or the life of the poet. *Birthday Letters* is positioned within this definition, and its value thereby assessed. According to this assessment the volume can finally be defined as poetry or as failing to be poetry. In each case 'poetry' or 'literature' itself is defined specifically and indeed exclusively in relation to the question of authorship. The question of literature, the question of the definition of literature and the judgement of literary value, finally turns on, finally turns to, the author.

THE QUESTION OF LITERATURE

This brief analysis of strategies of contemporary literary reviewing suggests that the question of the author is bound up with the 'question of literature', and that asking 'what is an author?' is intimately related to the question 'what is literature?' As Wordsworth and Coleridge surmised at the beginning of the nineteenth century, attempting to answer one question helps us to think about the other. It is possible, in other words, that by putting these questions together we might begin to approach an understanding not of what an author *is* so much as the contingency, the variability and the apparitional nature of authorship, as well as its centrality with respect to the 'institution' of criticism and theory. To end this book I want to consider two related ways of conceiving literature: through its relationship with fiction or fictionality in the first place, and by means of a thinking of its 'exemplary' status in the second. Addressing these questions, I propose, might help us to conceive of the specificity of the 'literary' author and to understand the 'crisis' that inhabits contemporary conceptions of the author as well as contemporary conceptions of literature, the crisis that indeed inhabits contemporary thinking of literature *as* a conception of authorship.

Contemplating the possibility of defining literature, Peggy Kamuf suggests that 'literary theory takes *fiction* seriously' and that what is characteristic of theory's engagement with fictionality is its sense that fiction involves an empty or hollow referentiality. 'A fiction refers to nothing that exists', Kamuf explains: 'It refers, but to nothing in existence.' 'Thus', she continues, 'the fictional act or operation consists in making reference but also in suspending the referent' (Kamuf 2002: 157, 159). Kamuf herself is here alluding, more or less explicitly, to Jacques Derrida's comments on literary reference in an interview with Derek Attridge entitled 'This Strange Institution Called Literature' (1992). Summarizing a lifetime's passion for literature, in this interview Derrida argues that

'There is no literature without a *suspended* relation to meaning and reference' and that 'suspended' means '*suspense*, but also *dependence*, condition, conditionality' (Derrida 1992: 48). Crucial to this claim is Derrida's sense that if literature involves a '*suspended* relation to meaning or reference' – where 'suspend' involves a state of 'indecision', a putting on hold, a temporary deferral – it also involves a relation of *dependency*, as when an addict is dependent on his drug, or, rather differently, perhaps, a bungee-jumper on his rubber cable: both are dependent, suspended, held up, kept from falling. So one way of thinking about literary texts, about the literariness of literary texts, one way of discriminating such texts from other discourses, other uses of language (scientific, philosophical, conversational, are Derrida's examples (Derrida 1992: 47)), is that they have this particular, duplicitous or double relation to meaning and reference. Literature both suspends reference and is dependent on it: this constitutes what Paul de Man calls the 'delicate and ever-suspended balance between reference and play that is the condition for aesthetic pleasure' (de Man 1986: 36). As Wallace Stevens has it, 'A poet's words are of *things* that do not exist without the words' (Stevens 1960: 32; italics added). Shakespeare refers to Prince Hamlet, for example, and Prince Hamlet has a historical existence outside of this gesture of reference (at least in Saxo's twelfth/thirteenth-century *History of the Danes* and in Scandinavian legend). But *Hamlet* also only refers to a figure contained by or articulated in the text, only to Shakespeare's Hamlet. To take a rather different example, Thomas Hardy refers to Dorset by 'fictionalizing' it as 'Wessex', and you can, as I did just the other day, visit 'Casterbridge' (Dorchester) or 'Budmouth' (Weymouth) in your car as well as in your imagination. But these places in fact have a strange – a 'fictional', as we call it – existence, denoted precisely by Hardy's names for them. In other words, you can get in your car and drive to Dorchester, but you might be disappointed to find that it is not Casterbridge, and not only because of the century and more since Hardy wrote a novel about its Mayor. Tess Durbeyfield was Agatha Thornycroft in so-called 'real life', as the *Dictionary of Real People and Places in Fiction* will inform you (Rintoul 1993: 54), but she is also only Tess Durbeyfield. And to take one final example, we can probably assume that despite similarities to various literary, historical and mythological personages, there is no individual that quite corresponds to Leopold Bloom in James Joyce's *Ulysses* (1922). But our pleasure in reading Joyce's novel is determined at least in part by our sense that Bloom could or might indeed have walked the Dublin streets on 16 June 1904; or, to think about it differently, that it makes little difference that he didn't and couldn't have because he didn't exist; or that an important part of reading the book involves the suspension of our disbelief that he did walk those streets. This is why J. Hillis Miller can define literature as 'a strange use of words to refer to things, people, and events about which it is impossible ever to know whether or not they have somewhere a latent existence' (Miller 2002: 45).

Something similar might be said about the author, about the author of a literary work, about the author in so much as he or she is conceived of *as author* of such a work. The author of *Tess of the D'Urbervilles*, for example, is both an individual who lived between 1840 and 1928, trained as an architect, lived most of his life in Dorset, married twice, at different times, two women called Emma (Gifford and Dugdale), and wrote seventeen novels, some forty short stories and more than nine hundred poems. But the author of *Tess of the D'Urbervilles* is also not that individual, or it is an individual as an empty shell, a hollow man, a man constructed or 'performed' in and by the novel. It is for this reason, perhaps, that if you do get in your car and drive to Dorchester in order to visit the museum there, with its prize exhibit, Hardy's study, or if you drive out to Higher Bockhampton nearby, to view the carefully preserved house in which Hardy was born, or even if you look around Max Gate, the house in which he lived for the last forty years of his life and in which he died, there will be something hollow in the experience. You will have witnessed what Alexander Nehemas calls the 'writer', or at least his accoutrements, his desk, his house, his books and pens, but not what Nehemas calls the 'author' (Nehemas 2002). The arch-sceptic theorist of authorship K.K. Ruthven would see it as a pointlessly naive journey: for him, such an attempt to connect with the author through an artefact amounts to an 'auratic experience for people who believe in contagious magic, and are thrilled by the apostolic experience of touching materials touched by famous people' (Ruthven 2001: 161). Much recent author theory has involved an attempt to make distinctions similar to Nehemas's, distinctions between the historical agent and the 'author-function', or 'artifical author' or 'author construct' or 'author-figure' or 'hypothetical author' or 'implied author' or 'postulated author' (see 'Appendix: An

Author Lexicon', below, for details). In some sense, the author of *Tess of the D'Urbervilles* is not the man who was born at Bockhampton, who lived, wrote and died at Max Gate, or who toyed with the pens so lovingly collected in Dorset County Museum. To put it perhaps more decisively, there is a relation of undecidability here: we cannot finally decide whether the author is that individual or an 'empty' gesture of reference, an uncanny gesture of reference that in fact alone constitutes the author.

As Nehemas puts it, in an essay that comes at the point from a some-what different direction, authors are not like fictional characters because they are 'not simply parts of texts'; but they are also not like 'actual writers' because they are 'not straightforwardly outside' those texts (Nehemas 2002: 100). Nehemas goes on to argue that the author is 'never depicted, but only exemplified, in a text', that she is a 'character manifested though not represented' in it (pp. 101, 106). The claim is perhaps related to E.M. Forster's celebration of anonymity, towards which, he argues, 'all literature tends': the authorial 'signature', Forster contends, 'merely distracts us from [a work's] true significance' (Forster 1951: 91–2). But this is not quite, or not always, true, and not quite true in an interesting way. If we take 'depicted' to include self-naming or 'autocitation' (Kimmelman 1999), then we can see that something odd, something uncanny, sometimes happens when authors break this rule, when they are indeed named or depicted *within* a text. It is unusual for an author to refer to himself by name within the literary or fictional realm of the text, but it is certainly not unheard of (see Curran 1999; Kimmelman 1999). Indeed, you could write a kind of history of European literature based on authors' internal acts of self-naming. Here are some examples. All we know of 'Hesiod' is that he is named as such at the beginning of 'Hesiod's' *Theogony*. To protect himself from plagiarism, the sixth-century BC poet Theognis signs his verse with a *sphragis* or 'seal', asserting that 'no one will choose the bad when better is to hand / and all will say, "This is Theognis' verse, / from Megara": my name is famous everywhere' (see Ford 1985). Virgil seals his *Georgics* with his name, Catullus names himself no less than twenty times in his poems, and Ovid (or Naso) opens Book 2 of the *Amores* with the promise of 'A second batch of verses by that naughty provincial poet, / Naso, the chronicler of his own / Wanton frivolities' (see Vickers 2002a: 511–14). Dante is named only once in the *Divine Comedy*, in the first words spoken by Beatrice to the besotted poet, when she tells him not to 'weep' for his guide Virgil's going – at the point, in other words, when Dante must stand on his own two authorial feet (*Purgatorio*, Canto xxx, ll. 55–6). Chaucer scathingly names himself in *The Man of Law's Prologue* ('Chaucer, thogh he kan but lewdly / On metres and on rymyng craftily' (ll. 47–8)), and he elsewhere characterizes his narrator, naming him 'Geffrey'; Thomas Hoccleve names himself in the 'Complaint' (ll. 1419–21); while William Langland's persona in *Piers Plowman* is named 'Will'. Will Shakespeare in turn makes a particular point of punning on his first name in the sonnets, and much has been made by certain kinds of critics of the inscription of a disseminated Shake-speare in the plays: 'Why write I still all one, ever the same, / And keep invention in a noted weed, / That every word doth almost tell my name . . . ?', Shakespeare asks knowingly in sonnet 76. Miguel de Cervantes's *Galatea* is one of the romances commented on in chapter 6 of Miguel de Cervantes's *Don Quixote*: 'That fellow Cervantes has been a good friend of mine for years', says the priest, 'and I know he's more conversant with adversity than with verse'. Ben Jonson movingly names both himself and his child, Ben Jonson, in his elegiac 'On My First Son': 'Rest in soft peace', Jonson says to his dead son, 'and, asked, say, here doth lie / Ben Jonson his best piece of poetry'. Alexander Pope understandably makes papal play of his own name in a number of poems, whereas, although he originally contemplated calling *Childe Harold's Pilgrimage Childe Burun's Pilgrimage* (employing an old spelling of his own name), Byron's name makes a perhaps surprisingly modest single appearance in his published poems. Samuel Taylor Coleridge, Robert Browning, and T.S. Eliot make light of their names in their light verse ('How unpleasant to meet Mr. Eliot!', Eliot declares, in 'Five-Finger Exercises'), but William Wordsworth rarely names himself in his poems, despite the paronomastic possibilities of Wordsworth that both Coleridge and Charles Lamb found irresistible. It is possible that James Joyce is evoked in Molly Bloom's confusion of Jesus with her maker, James, in *Ulysses* ('O Jamesy'), and his name appears to be scrambled with that of Euclid's *Elements of Geometry*, as 'elementator joyclid', in *Finnegans Wake*. The narrator of Proust's apparently autobiographical novel *À la recherche du temps perdu* has his author's first name, Marcel. 'Ballard', whose first name is 'James', is both a character in and first-person narrator of J.G. Ballard's *Crash*. Paul Auster is a character in Paul Auster's *City of Glass*. Salman Rushdie famously made controversial, and potentially lethal, use of his own first name in *The Satanic Verses* for a character who happens to be a writer, a scurrilously inaccurate scribe (as well as depicting God in terms that critics have not failed to recognize as Rushdie himself: 'of medium height, fairly heavily built, with salt-and-pepper beard cropped close to the line of the jaw', God, like Rushdie, is balding, seems to have dandruff, and wears glasses (Rushdie 1988: 318)). And in one of my favourite examples, the contemporary poet Michael Ayres names himself in a disconcerting but not unreasonable warning to his reader in his long, searingly autographic poem 'Transporter': 'don't be Michael Ayres', he advises us – as if without the warning we would, or would try to, be him (Ayres 2003: 55).

There is a certain strangeness, something uncanny, in many of these nominal appearances of authors within texts and, in a remarkable early work on the 'Author and Hero in Aesthetic Activity' (c.1920–3), the Soviet critic and theorist M.M. Bakhtin helps us to understand why such namings are disconcerting: 'The author must be situated on the boundary of the world he is bringing into being as the active creator of this world', Bakhtin declares, 'for his intrusion into that world destroys its aesthetic stability' (Bakhtin 1990: 191). But I want to suggest that it is precisely this 'destruction of aesthetic stability' that may be said at least in part to constitute the literariness of literary texts and that the strange, the uncanny appearance of the author's name in a work might help to account for the difficulty we have in accounting for authors of literary texts more generally, as well as for our fascination with those figures. Such examples suggest that the 'crisis' of literary criticism and theory, the crisis that literary studies just *is*, just has to be, revolves around the question of what an 'author' is.

My second, closely related point concerns the example. A traditional way of discriminating literary texts from other kinds of discourses is to say that a poem or novel or play has a certain specificity, that it is 'unique', *and* that it has, at the same time, a certain generality, that it is 'universal' or 'universalizable'. There is from the first, in fact, the problem or question or dilemma of exemplarity, there is the question of the way in which the institution of literature has presented literary texts as uncannily exemplary, the way in which such texts are held to involve a 'universalizable singularity' (Derrida 2000: 94). Timothy Clark, for example, has recently argued that literary language 'puts to work an undecidability about the status of its language which both compels and resists interpretation' and that this undecidability is a function of the way that literary language productively 'skews' the 'distinctions between the verbal and the conceptual', generating 'an aporetic relation between the singular and the universal'. Clark offers as an example the word 'visage' in *Hamlet*, and asks whether 'its occurrence is to be taken under some more general conceptual framework', whether it 'subserves several distinct concepts', or whether the word could just as well be substituted by the word 'face', say, 'without significant loss' (Clark 2002: 100). Clark's example of 'visage' in *Hamlet*, and his sense of our permanent, our proper indecision over whether it is a word or a concept, can be related to the way in which 'Shakespeare' may be said both to name a particular individual, a person, an identity, and to name no one but to denote instead a certain unifying and meaning-making principle or 'function'.

The idea that literature has a strange relationship with exemplarity, with singularity *and* universality, in fact goes back as far as the beginning of Western literary theory: it is established with the institution of literary theory, and therefore of literature itself, in the *Poetics* (*c.*330 BC). Aristotle argues that 'it is the function of a poet to relate not things that have happened, but things that may happen, i.e. that are possible in accordance with probability or necessity'. This is in contrast to the historian, who 'relates things that have happened'. Aristotle argues that poetry is therefore 'a more philosophical and more serious thing than history' since 'poetry tends to speak of universals, history of particulars' (Aristotle 2001: 97–8). He then qualifies this claim by explaining that there is of course nothing to stop a poet representing something that has happened, since something that has happened is, by definition, possible (p. 98). But the claim also makes it clear that poetry is not, not quite, philosophy: poetry is 'more philosophical', Aristotle says, not that it is philosophy. This crucial – and highly influential – distinction between literature, history and philosophy is usefully elaborated by Sir Philip Sidney in *An Apology for Poetry*. The philosopher's knowledge, Sidney says,

> standeth so upon the abstract and general, that happy is that man who may understand him, and more happy that can apply what he doth understand. On the other side, the historian, wanting the precept, is so tied, not to what should be but to what is, to the particular truth of

things and not the general reason of things, that his example draweth no necessary consequence, and therefore a less fruitful doctrine.

Now doth the peerless poet perform both: for whatsoever the philosopher saith should be done, he giveth a perfect picture of it in some one by whom he presupposeth it was done, so as he coupleth the general notion with the particular example.

(Sidney 2002: 90)

The point is that poetry is the kind of writing that inhabits an uncertain space somewhere between the specificity of history and the generality of philosophy. Poetry is not history, since it is more 'philosophical', more theoretical, more generalizing, than that. But it is also not philosophy, since it involves the recounting of particular events rather than, or in addition to, the statement of 'universal' truths. Or, rather, in as much as poetry can be said to involve statements of such truths it does so by means of specific events, occurrences, characters, and through an emphasis on the specificity, the untranslatability, of language.

To take a familar example, John Keats's 'Ode on a Grecian Urn' (1820) ends with two evocative and troublingly generalizing last lines:

'Beauty is truth, truth beauty' – that is all
   Ye know on earth, and all ye need to know.

Much ink – too much ink – has been spilt over these words as critics try to work out who is speaking here, whether a general or only a local, a particular proposition is involved, whether the statement can be said to be undermined by authorial or narratorial or poetic irony, and indeed whether the statement is in fact true. But in truth it may be that these questions can never be resolved since the statement is both a general, universalizing statement – indeed, it asserts itself as such – and part of a poem, with its own specificity, its own mode of being, and including its own particular strategies of indirection. And the status of this example as an example is itself part of the problem. Whatever we say about the ending to Keats's poem can be construed as both a statement about the singularity of an individual speech act *and* a more general illustration or example of a general literary principle. It used to be said with tedious regularity that you should not generalize about literature: indeed, didn't William Blake warn us, idiotically, that 'To Generalize is to be an Idiot' (Blake 1965: 630)? This has always been one of the reasons adduced for not doing literary theory. But perhaps the declaration should be modified: perhaps we should say that you cannot make general statements about literary texts, that you cannot generalize from them, and that you must. Here, therefore, is an example of a general statement about literary texts, perhaps the only one we can make: every literary text is, or aspires to be, both unique, singular, and general. Literature, we might say, is, in an uncanny, undecidable way, exemplary. Its language is both 'verbal' and 'conceptual'. It both can and cannot be translated. That – all of that – is what is literary about a literary text.

Aristotle, then, suggests that poetry involves a peculiar, indeed an aporetic relationship between the particular and the universal. Although terms vary, many literary theorists have dwelled on just this oddness of the literary work: as W.K. Wimsatt commented fifty years ago, 'literary theorists have from early times to the present' argued that 'a work of literary art is in some peculiar sense a very individual or a very universal thing or both' (Wimsatt 1954: 69). Derrida takes this tradition and gives it a particular, a Derridean, twist or spin. 'Something of literature will have begun', he proposes, 'when it is not possible to decide whether, when I speak of something, I am speaking of something (of the thing itself, this one, for itself) or if I am giving an example, an example of something or an example of the fact that I can speak of something' (Derrida 1995: 142–3). When Hardy speaks of Tess, we might ask, does he mean to speak of an individual, or does he mean to give us an example of certain kinds of individuals, of certain kinds of actions, certain kinds of thoughts, motives, fears, desires, wishes, dreams? Derrida's position entails the proposition that to resolve this question would be precisely to dissolve what it is about Hardy's novel that makes it literary, would be to dissolve its literary force, its literary effect and its literary effectiveness.

The same can be said of the author as framed or conceived within the institution of literature: the author is both him- or herself, individual, unique, a one-off and at the same time, *as author*, more than this, a general or 'universal' figure, a figure that goes beyond its own genesis, its own origins in and as a particular, unique individual: the author 'is more type than man, more passion than type', Yeats declares (Yeats 1994: 204). This, in effect, is what Immanuel Kant maintains is the 'exemplary originality' of the 'genius', in *The Critique of Judgement* (1790) (Kant 1952: 181; see Attridge 2004: 35–7). As Seán Burke comments, rather doubtfully, in the course of his somewhat exorbitant reading of Derrida's *Of Grammatology*, 'Doubtless the problem of exemplarity is one facet of the problem of the author' (Burke 1998: 137). We might go further. There is no doubt, we might say, that the problem of exemplarity is fundamental to the question of authorship in and as the question of literature. And this might explain the unease of Ted Hughes's reviewers and why Barthes (even Barthes, especially Barthes) reserves a certain desire for the author, needs him or her when he talks about 'the pleasure of the text', about the pleasure that he gets from literary texts: 'in a way, I desire the author: I need his figure . . . as he needs mine' (Barthes 1975: 27). And it might explain, finally, why the enduring power of literary texts, a power that recent criticism and theory have so often resisted or denied, is to encourage our identifications not only with characters but with these strangers, these others, these authors.

Literature raises the question of the author, as if from the dead. The crisis of authorship is, in the end, the crisis of literature. What critics talk about when they talk about literature is the problem of authorship. To put this differently, we might say that critical interest in literature is driven by an uncertainty about the author, about what the author is, about what *this* author is (this author that we are reading, now, a book in our hands). And such an interest is impelled in fact by the author's irresistible infraction of the limits of textuality, meaning, intention. The condition of literary criticism and theory, the condition on which criticism and theory are undertaken, the condition even of reading, is this crisis, this crisis of literature, this uncanny, undecidable author.

APPENDIX: AN AUTHOR LEXICON

Apparitional author
Artificial author
Auctor
Auteur
Author
~~Author~~
Author construct
Author-effect
Author figure
Author-function
Bard
Created author
Creative author
Dramatist
Founder of discursivity
Fundamental author
Hack
Historical author
Hypothetical author

Implied author
Modern author
Novelist
Phantasmatic author
Playwright
Poet
Postulated author
Prophet
Pseudo-historical author
Romantic author
Scribbler
Scribe
Script writer
Scriptor
Singer
Troubadour
Urauthor
Vates
Writer

This author lexicon lists some of the ways in which writers, critics and theorists have tried to name the individual who writes or composes, or the image of that individual presented by literary texts. In what follows, I have attempted briefly to group the terms and to explain how they are used.

- Many of the terms listed above originate in twentieth-century literary criticism and theory. Some are specifically designed to discriminate differently conceived personalities or personae from the historical agent(s) who produce the text, from what Jorge Gracia calls the **historical author**, what Alexander Nehemas calls the **writer** or what H.L. Hix calls the **creative author**. Wayne Booth was the first to offer a term for the authorial figure as distinct from the historical author in his term **implied author** in *The Rhetoric of Fiction* (1961). Critics and theorists have since multiplied such figures or fictions of authorship, giving them a variety of names in order to attempt more precisely to designate the workings of author-figures within texts: William Gass refers to the **artificial author** (see Gass 1985: 283), William Irwin to the **author construct**, Nehemas to the **author figure** and to the **postulated author**, Jerrold Levinson to the **hypothetical author**, Couturier and Ruthven to the **author-effect**, Hix to the **created author**.

- Another group of terms goes beyond a constructed author or author-figure within the text but retains a distinction between what can be known or hypothesized about an author and the historical individual that produced the text: Gracia refers to the **pseudo-historical author** and Irwin to the **urauthor**. Related to these figures is Michel Foucault's notion of the **author-function**.

- A third category attempts to dislodge our sense of the distinction between a 'fictional' author and the 'real' author, to suggest that one of the important effects of authorship is to produce an uncertainty of authorship, an uncertainty about his or her 'presence' in a text: Timothy Clark refers to the **phantasmatic author** (Clark 1997: 26) and a term I have used is the **apparitional author**.

- The term **author** itself is both a general category to cover all these terms, and at the same time an ideological construct which is held to be most fully expressed in the Romantic period: this latter sense of the author (sometimes called the post-medieval or **Romantic** or **modern author**) is an autonomous individual who expresses his or her original thoughts, desires, wishes, ideas in a text.

- Other terms are explicitly designed to resist or refute such an ideology: Roland Barthes uses the term **scriptor** to attempt to avoid the implications of autonomy, expressiveness, individuality and originality often assigned to authors (Barthes 1995); William Gass places the word under erasure (~~author~~) (Gass 1985: 285); and the word **writer** is often used to serve a similar purpose. While **scribe** is normally conceived of as a medieval amanuensis or clerk, a copyist, it can also refer more generally to a writer, the distinction between copying and originating writing being less clear-cut in the medieval period than it has since become.

- Other terms are designed actively to denigrate certain kinds of authorship, particularly writing for money (**hack**) and certain forms of amateurism or certain levels of (in)competence (**scribbler**).

- Some of these terms make generic distinctions between different kinds of authorship: **dramatist**, **playwright**, **novelist**, **poet** and **script writer** each have their own history and their own specificity. **Poet** was probably the most common general term for the literary author before the beginning of the nineteenth century.

- The French word *auteur* is used to designate the supposedly single originating agent (usually the director) in the context of cinema, a designation which also serves to distinguish 'art films' from less aesthetically prestigious and more populist 'Hollywood' films.
- The **founder of discursivity** (sometimes called the **fundamental author**) is Michel Foucault's quite specialized term for the (non-literary) writer who 'founds' a discourse (his examples are Marx and Freud).
- *Auctor* is the medieval term out of which the modern English word 'author' develops. The *auctor* is endowed with *auctoritas*, authority: the fundamental quality of the medieval *auctor* is to speak the truth and, as such, the *auctor* is significantly different from the post-medieval conception of the author (the post-medieval author may or may not speak the truth).
- **Singer** is used by some critics to refer to oral epic poets – Homer being the preeminent example in the Western literary tradition – who composed as they performed, and performed in a chant-like singing to a basic musical accompaniment.
- **Troubadour** is a poet, usually aristocratic and usually speaking of love, prominent in Spain, Italy and France in the eleventh to thirteenth centuries.
- Finally, **vates**, **bard** and **prophet** are terms which, in the past, have awarded authors – poets in particular – a certain status within society, one allied with a mystical, priestly ability to foresee the future and to tell fundamental truths to and about their society.

BIBLIOGRAPHY

Abrams, M.H. (1953) *The Mirror and the Lamp: Romantic Theory and the Critical Tradition*, New York, Oxford University Press.

Aristotle (2001) *Poetics*, in Vincent B. Leitch (ed.) *The Norton Anthology of Theory and Criticism*, New York, Norton, pp. 90–117.

Ashbery, John (2000) *Other Traditions*, Cambridge, Mass., Harvard University Press.

Attridge, Derek (2004) *The Singularity of Literature*, London, Routledge.

Ayres, Michael (2003) *a.m.*, Cambridge, Salt.

Bain, Alexander (1869) 'On Teaching English', *The Fortnightly Review*, ns 31 (July): 200–14.

Bakhtin, M.M. (1990) 'Author and Hero in Aesthetic Activity', in Michael Holquist and Vadim Liapunov (eds) *Art and Answerability: Early Philosophical Essays*, Austin, University of Texas Press, pp. 4–236.

Baldick, Chris (1983) *The Social Mission of English Criticism, 1848–1932*, Oxford, Clarendon Press.

Ballard, J.G. (1990) *Crash*, London, Grafton Books.

Barthes, Roland (1974) *S/Z*, trans. Richard Miller, London, Cape.

—— (1975) *The Pleasure of the Text*, trans. Richard Miller, New York, The Noonday Press.

—— (1977a) *Sade, Fourier, Loyola*, trans. Richard Miller, London, Jonathan Cape.

—— (1977b) *Roland Barthes by Roland Barthes*, trans. Richard Howard, New York, Hill and Wang.

—— (1979) 'From Work to Text', in Josué V. Harari (ed.) *Textual Strategies: Perspectives in Post-Structuralist Criticism*, London, Methuen, pp. 73–81.

—— (1981) 'Theory of the Text', in Robert Young (ed.) *Untying the Text: A Post-structuralist Reader*, London, Routledge and Kegan Paul, pp. 31–47.

—— (1993–5) *Oeuvres Complètes*, ed. Éric Marty, 3 vols, Paris, Editions du Seuil.

—— (1995) 'The Death of the Author', in Seán Burke (ed.) *Authorship: From Plato to Postmodernism: A Reader*, Edinburgh, Edinburgh University Press, pp. 125–30.

Bate, Jonathan (1989) 'Shakespeare and Original Genius', in Penelope Murray (ed.) *Genius: The History of an Idea*, Oxford, Basil Blackwell, pp. 76–97.

—— (2003) 'Navigate the Circus of Fancy with Fact', *The Times Higher Education Supplement* 1,600 (1 August): 22–3.

Beal, Peter (1998) *In Praise of Scribes: Manuscripts and their Makers in Seventeenth-Century England*, Oxford, Clarendon Press.

Beardsley, Monroe, C. (1970) 'The Authority of the Text', in *The Possibilities of Criticism*, Detroit, Wayne State University Press.

—— (1982) 'Intentions and Interpretations', in *The Aesthetic Point of View: Selected Essays*, ed. Michael J. Wreen and Donald M. Callen, Ithaca, Cornell University Press, pp. 188–207.

Bénichou, Paul (1999) *The Consecration of the Writer, 1780–1830*, trans. Mark K. Jensen, Lincoln, University of Nebraska Press.

Benjamin, Walter (2001) 'The Work of Art in the Age of Mechanical Reproduction', in Vincent B. Leitch (ed.) *The Norton Anthology of Theory and Criticism*, New York, Norton, pp. 1166–86.

Bennett, Andrew (1999) *Romantic Poets and the Culture of Posterity*, Cambridge, Cambridge University Press.

—— (2005a) 'The Idea of the Author', in Nicholas Roe (ed.) *Romanticism: An Oxford Guide*, Oxford, Oxford University Press.

—— (2005b) 'The Romantic Author', in Patricia Waugh (ed.) *The Theory and Practice of Literary Criticism: An Oxford Guide*, Oxford, Oxford University Press.

Biriotti, Maurice and Nicola Miller (eds) (1993) *What is an Author?*, Manchester, Manchester University Press.

Bissell, Elizabeth Beaumont (ed.) (2002) *The Question of Literature: The Place of the Literary in Contemporary Theory*, Manchester, Manchester University Press.

Blake, William (1965) *The Poetry and Prose of William Blake*, ed. David V. Erdman, New York, Doubleday.

Booth, Wayne C. (1961) *The Rhetoric of Fiction*, Chicago, University of Chicago Press.

Bourdieu, Pierre (1993) *The Field of Cultural Production: Essays on Art and Literature*, ed. Randall Johnson, New York, Columbia University Press.

—— (1996) *The Rules of Art: Genesis and Structure of the Literary Field*, trans. Susan Emanuel, Stanford, Stanford University Press.

Bristol, Michael D. (1999) 'Shakespeare: The Myth', in David Scott Kastan (ed.) *A Companion to Shakespeare*, Oxford, Blackwell, pp. 489–502.

Brooks, Cleanth (1998) 'The Formalist Critics', in Julie Rivkin and Michael Ryan (eds) *Literary Theory: An Anthology*, Oxford, Blackwell, pp. 52–7.

Brown, Gregory S. (2003) 'Authorship', in Alan Charles Kors (ed.) *Encyclopedia of the Enlightenment*, vol. 1, Oxford, Oxford University Press, pp. 103–8.

Burke, Seán (ed.) (1995) *Authorship: From Plato to Postmodernism: A Reader*, Edinburgh, Edinburgh University Press.

—— (1998) *The Death and Return of the Author: Criticism and Subjectivity in Barthes, Foucault and Derrida*, 2nd edn, Edinburgh, Edinburgh University Press.

—— (2002) 'The Biographical Imperative', *Essays in Criticism* 52, 3: 191–208.

Burrow, J.A. (1982) *Medieval Writers and Their Work: Middle English Literature and its Background, 1100–1500*, Oxford, Oxford University Press.

Burrow, Colin (1998) 'Life and Work in Shakespeare's Poems', *Proceedings of the British Academy* 97: 15–50.

Butler, Judith (1990) *Gender Trouble: Feminism and the Subversion of Identity*, New York, Routledge.

Carver, Raymond (1988) 'A Conversation with Kasia Boddy', *London Review of Books* 10, 16 (15 September): 16.

Caughie, John (ed.) (1981) *Theories of Authorship: A Reader*, London, Routledge and Kegan Paul.

Chartier, Roger (1994) *The Order of Books: Readers, Authors, and Libraries in Europe* between the Fourteenth and Eighteenth Centuries, trans. Lydia G. Cochrane, Stanford, Stanford University Press.

Cixous, Hélène (1997) 'The Laugh of the Medusa', in Robyn R. Warhol and Diane Price Herndl (eds) Feminisms: An Anthology of Literary Theory and Criticism, Basingstoke, Macmillan, pp. 347–62.

Clark, Timothy (1997) The Theory of Inspiration: Composition as a Crisis of Subjectivity in Romantic and Post-Romantic Writing, Manchester, Manchester University Press.

—— (2002) 'Literary Force, Institutional Values', in Elizabeth Beaumont Bissell (ed.) The Question of Literature : The Place of the Literary in Contemporary Theory, Manchester, Manchester University Press, pp. 91–104.

Clery, E.J., Caroline Franklin and Peter Garside (eds) (2002) Authorship, Commerce and the Public: Scenes of Writing, 1750–1850, Basingstoke, Palgrave Macmillan.

Close, Anthony (1990) 'The Empirical Author: Salman Rushdie's The Satanic Verses', Philosophy and Literature 14, 2: 248–67.

Coleman, Patrick, Jayne Lewis and Jill Kowalik (eds) (2000) Representations of the Self from the Renaissance to Romanticism, Cambridge, Cambridge University Press.

Coleridge, Samuel Taylor (1983) Biographia Literaria, ed. James Engell and W. Jackson Bate, 2 vols, London, Routledge and Kegan Paul.

—— (1987) Lectures 1808–1819 On Literature, ed. R.A. Foakes, 2 vols, London, Routledge and Kegan Paul.

Collins, A.S. (1927) Authorship in the Days of Johnson: Being a Study of the Relation Between Author, Patron, Publisher and Public, 1726–1780, London, Robert Holden.

—— (1928) The Profession of Letters: A Study of the Relation of Author to Patron, Publisher, and Public, 1780–1832, London, George Routledge.

Corrigan, Timothy (2003) 'The Commerce of Auteurism', in Virginia Wright Wexman (ed.) Film and Authorship, New Brunswick, Rutgers University Press, pp. 96–111.

Couturier, Maurice (1995) La Figure de l'auteur, Paris, Éditions du Seuil.

—— (1999) 'The Near-Tyranny of the Author: "Pale Fire"', in Julian W. Connolly (ed.) Nabakov and His Fictions: New Perspectives, Cambridge, Cambridge University Press, pp. 54–72.

Crane, Mary Thomas (2001) Shakespeare's Brain: Reading with Cognitive Theory, Princeton, Princeton University Press.

Crawford, Robert (2001) The Modern Poet: Poetry, Academia, and Knowledge since the 1750s, Oxford, Oxford University Press.

Crewe, Jonathan (1990) Trials of Authorship: Anterior Forms and Poetic Reconstruction from Wyatt to Shakespeare, Berkeley, University of California Press.

Curran, Stuart (1999) 'Romantic Women Poets: Inscribing the Self', in Isobel Armstrong and Virginia Blain (eds) Women's Poetry in the Enlightenment: The Making of a Canon, 1730–1820, Basingstoke, Macmillan, pp. 145–66.

Currie, Gregory (2003) 'Interpretation in Art', in Jerrold Levinson (ed.) The Oxford Handbook of Aesthetics, Oxford, Oxford University Press, pp. 291–306.

Davis, Oliver (2002) 'The Author at Work in Genetic Criticism', *Paragraph* 25: 92–106.

De Grazia, Margreta (1991) *Shakespeare Verbatim: The Reproduction of Authenticity and the 1790 Apparatus*, Oxford, Clarendon Press.

De Man, Paul (1986) *The Resistance to Theory*, Manchester, Manchester University Press.

Derrida, Jacques (1976) *Of Grammatology*, trans. Gayatri Chakravorty Spivak, Baltimore, Johns Hopkins University Press.

—— (1978) *Writing and Difference*, trans. Alan Bass, London, Routledge.

—— (1983) 'The Time of a Thesis: Punctuations', in *Philosophy in France Today*, ed. Alan Montefiore, Cambridge, Cambridge University Press, pp. 34–50.

—— (1984) *Signéponge/Signsponge*, trans. Richard Rand, New York, Columbia University Press.

—— (1988a) *The Ear of the Other: Otobiography, Transference, Translation*, ed. Christie McDonald, Lincoln, University of Nebraska Press.

—— (1988b) *Limited Inc*, ed. Gerald Graff, Evanston, Ill., Northwestern University Press.

—— (1992) 'This Strange Institution Called Literature: An Interview with Jacques Derrida', in *Acts of Literature*, ed. Derek Attridge, London, Routledge, pp. 33–75.

—— (1995) *On the Name*, ed. Thomas Dutoit, Stanford, Stanford University Press.

—— (2000) *Demeure: Fiction and Testimony*, trans. Elizabeth Rottenberg, Stanford, Stanford University Press.

—— (2002) *Without Alibi*, trans. Peggy Kamuf, Stanford, Stanford University Press.

Dickie, George and Kent Wilson (1995) 'The Intentional Fallacy: Defending Beardsley', *Journal of Aesthetics and Art Criticism*, 53: 133–50.

Dobranski, Stephen B. (1999) *Milton, Authorship, and the Book Trade*, Cambridge, Cambridge University Press.

Dobson, Michael (1992) *The Making of the National Poet: Shakespeare, Adaptation and Authorship, 1660–1769*, Oxford, Clarendon Press.

Dunn, Kevin (1994) *Pretexts of Authority: The Rhetoric of Authorship in the Renaissance Preface*, Stanford, Stanford University Press.

Dunn, Douglas (2000) 'A Difficult, Simple Art', in W.N. Herbert and Matthew Hollis (eds) *Strong Words: Modern Poets on Modern Poetry*, Tarset, Northumberland, Bloodaxe Books, pp. 163–6.

Dutton, Denis (1987) 'Why Intentionalism Won't Go Away', in Anthony J. Cascardi (ed.) *Literature and the Question of Philosophy*, Baltimore, Johns Hopkins University Press, pp. 192–209.

Eagleton, Terry (1990) *The Ideology of the Aesthetic*, Oxford, Basil Blackwell.

Eichenbaum, Boris (1998) 'Introduction to the Formal Method', in Julie Rivkin and Michael Ryan (eds) *Literary Theory: An Anthology*, Oxford, Blackwell, pp. 8–16.

Eisenstein, Elizabeth (1979) *The Printing Press as an Agent of Change: Communications and Cultural Transformations in Early-Modern Europe*, 2 vols, Cambridge, Cambridge University Press.

Eliot, T.S. (1975) *Selected Prose*, ed. Frank Kermode, London, Faber and Faber.

Ellmann, Maud (1987) *The Poetics of Impersonality: T.S. Eliot and Ezra Pound*, Brighton, Harvester.

Epstein, William (ed.) (1991) *Contesting the Subject*, West Lafayette, Ind., Purdue University Press.

Erdman, David V. and Ephim G. Fogel (eds) (1966) *Evidence for Authorship: Essays on Problems of Attribution*, Ithaca, Cornell University Press.

Erickson, Lee (2002) '"Unboastful Bard": Originally Anonymous English Romantic Poetry Book Publication, 1770–1835', *New Literary History* 33: 247–78.

Everett, Barbara (2003) 'Alphabeted', *London Review of Books* 25, 15 (7 August): 6–10.

Ezell, Margaret J.M. (1999) *Social Authorship and the Advent of Print*, Baltimore, Johns Hopkins University Press.

Faulkner, William (1977) *Selected Letters*, ed. Joseph Blotner, London, Scolar.

Feather, John (1994) *Publishing, Piracy and Politics: An Historical Survey of Copyright in Britain*, London, Mansell.

Feinstein, Elaine (2001) *Ted Hughes: The Life of a Poet*, New York, Norton.

Feldman, Paula R. (2002) 'Women Poets and Anonymity in the Romantic Era', *New Literary History* 33: 279–89.

Felman, Shoshana (1993) *What Does a Woman Want? Reading and Sexual Difference*, Baltimore, Johns Hopkins University Press.

Felski, Rita (2003) *Literature After Feminism*, Chicago, Chicago University Press.

Ferry, Anne (2002) 'Anonymity: The Literary History of a Word', *New Literary History* 33: 193–214.

Fineman, Joel (1991) *The Subjectivity Effect in Western Literary Tradition*, Cambridge, Mass., MIT Press.

Finkelstein, David and Alistair McCleery (eds) (2002) *The Book History Reader*, London, Routledge.

Fish, Stanley (1982) 'With the Compliments of the Author: Reflections on Austin and Derrida', *Critical Inquiry* 8: 693–721.

Flaubert, Gustave (1980) *The Letters of Gustave Flaubert, 1830–1857*, ed. Francis Steegmuller, Cambridge, Mass., Harvard University Press.

Folkenflik, Robert (1981) 'The Artist as Hero in the Eighteenth Century', *The Year's Work in English Studies* 12: 91–108.

Ford, Andrew L. (1985) 'The Seal of Theognis: The Politics of Authorship in Archaic Greece', in Thomas J. Figueira and Gregory Nagy (eds) *Theognis of Megara: Poetry and the Polis*, Baltimore, Johns Hopkins University Press, pp. 82–95.

Forster, E.M. (1951) 'Anonymity: An Enquiry', in *Two Cheers for Democracy*, London, Edward Arnold, pp. 87–97.

Foster, Don (2001) *Author Unknown: On the Trail of Anonymous*, London, Macmillan.

Foucault, Michel (1979) 'What is an Author?', in Josué V. Harari (ed.) *Textual Strategies: Perspectives in Post-Structuralist Criticism*, London, Methuen, pp. 141–60.

—— (1981) *The History of Sexuality: An Introduction*, trans. Robert Hurley, Harmondsworth, Penguin.

Frost, Robert (2000) 'The Figure a Poem Makes', in W.N. Herbert and Matthew Hollis (eds) *Strong Words: Modern Poets on Modern Poetry*, Tarset, Northumberland, Bloodaxe Books, pp. 44–6.

Gallagher, Catherine and Stephen Greenblatt (2000) *Practicing New Historicism*, Chicago, University of Chicago Press.

Garber, Marjorie (1987) *Shakespeare's Ghost Writers: Literature as Uncanny Causality*, New York, Methuen.

Gass, William H. (1985) 'The Death of the Author', in *Habitations of the Word: Essays*, New York, Simon and Schuster, pp. 265–87.

Gerard, Alexander (1961) 'An Essay on Genius', in *Eighteenth-Century Critical Essays*, ed. Scott Elledge, Ithaca, Cornell University Press, pp. 882–913.

Gerstner, David A. and Janet Staiger (eds) (2003) *Authorship and Film*, New York, Routledge.

Gibbons, Reginald (ed.) (1979) *The Poet's Work: 29 Poets on the Origins and Practice of Their Art*, Chicago, University of Chicago Press.

Gilbert, Sandra M. and Susan Gubar (1979) *The Madwoman in the Attic: The Woman Writer and the Nineteenth-Century Literary Imagination*, New Haven, Yale University Press.

Glover, Michael (1998) 'Into the Open', *New Statesman* 11, 489 (30 January): 45.

Goldhill, Simon (1991) *The Poet's Voice: Essays on Poetics and Greek Literature*, Cambridge, Cambridge University Press.

Gracia, Jorge J.E. (2002) 'A Theory of the Author', in William Irwin (ed.) *The Death and Resurrection of the Author?*, Westport, Conn., Greenwood Press, pp. 161–90.

Graham, W.S. (2000) 'Notes on a Poetry of Release', in W.N. Herbert and Matthew Hollis (eds) *Strong Words: Modern Poets on Modern Poetry*, Tarset, Northumberland, Bloodaxe Books, pp. 117–21.

Graziosi, Barbara (2002) *Inventing Homer: The Early Reception of Epic*, Cambridge, Cambridge University Press.

Greenblatt, Stephen (1980) *Renaissance Self-Fashioning: From More to Shakespeare*, Chicago, University of Chicago Press.

—— (1988) *Shakespearean Negotiations: The Circulation of Social Energy in Renaissance England*, Oxford, Clarendon Press.

—— (1990) *Learning to Curse: Essays in Early Modern Culture*, New York, Routledge.

—— (2001) *Hamlet in Purgatory*, Princeton, Princeton University Press.

Greetham, D.C. (1999) *Theories of the Text*, Oxford, Oxford University Press.

Grice, H.P. (1971) 'Intention and Uncertainty', *Proceedings of the British Academy* 57: 263–79.

Griffin, Robert J. (1999) 'Anonymity and Authorship', *New Literary History*, 30: 877–95.

Griffin, Jasper (2000) 'Introduction', in Homer, *The Odyssey*, trans. Martin Hammond, London, Duckworth, pp. xiii–xxvi.

Hadfield, Andrew (1997) *Edmund Spenser's Irish Experience: Wilde Fruit and Salvage Soyl*, Oxford, Clarendon Press.

Hamilton, Ian (1998) 'A Mismatched Marriage', *The Sunday Telegraph, Sunday Review* (25 January): 7.

Hammond, Brean S. (1997) *Professional Imaginative Writing in England, 1670–1740: 'Hackney for Bread'*, Oxford, Clarendon Press.

Hanson, Elizabeth (1998) *Discovering the Subject in Renaissance England*, Cambridge, Cambridge University Press.

Harris, V. Wendell (1996) *Literary Meaning: Reclaiming the Study of Literature*, London, Macmillan.

Hazlitt, William (1930–4) *The Complete Works of William Hazlitt*, 21 vols, ed. P.P. Howe, London, Dent.

Heale, Elizabeth (2003) *Autobiography and Authorship in Renaissance Verse: Chronicles of the Self*, Basingstoke, Palgrave.

Heaney, Seamus (1998) 'A Wounded Power Rises from the Depths', *The Irish Times, Weekend Books* (31 January): 11.

Helgerson, Richard (1983) *Self-Crowned Laureates: Spenser, Jonson, Milton and the Literary System*, Berkeley, University of California Press.

Herbert, W.N. and Matthew Hollis (eds) (2000) *Strong Words: Modern Poets on Modern Poetry*, Tarset, Northumberland, Bloodaxe Books.

Hirsch, E.D., Jr. (1967) *Validity in Interpretation*, New Haven, Yale University Press.

—— (1976) *The Aims of Interpretation*, Chicago, University of Chicago Press.

—— (1984) 'Meaning and Significance Reinterpreted', *Critical Inquiry* 11: 202–25.

—— (1994) 'Transhistorical Intentions and the Persistence of Allegory', *New Literary History* 25: 549–67.

Hirschfeld, Heather (2001) 'Early Modern Collaboration and Theories of Authorship', *PMLA* 116, 3: 609–22.

Hix, H.L. (1990) *Morte d'Author: An Autopsy*, Philadelphia, Temple University Press.

Hobby, Elaine (1988) *Virtue of Necessity: English Women's Writing, 1649–1688*, London, Virago.

Hofkosh, Sonia (1998) *Sexual Politics and the Romantic Author*, Cambridge, Cambridge University Press.

Holmes, Olivia (2000) *Assembling the Lyric Self: Authorship from Troubadour Song to Italian Poetry Book*, Minneapolis, University of Minnesota Press.

Holt, Jason (2002) 'The Marginal Life of the Author', in William Irwin (ed.) *The Death and Resurrection of the Author?*, Westport, Conn., Greenwood Press, pp. 65–78.

Howard, Jean E. (1986) 'The New Historicism in Renaissance Studies', *English Literary Renaissance* 16: 13–43.

Inge, M. Thomas (2001) 'Collaboration and Concepts of Authorship', *PMLA* 116, 3: 623–30.

Irigaray, Luce (1985) *This Sex Which is Not One*, trans. Catherine Porter, Ithaca, Cornell University Press.

Irwin, William (1999) *Intentionalist Interpretation: A Philosophical Explanation and Defense*, Westport, Conn., Greenwood Press.

——— (ed.) (2002a) *The Death and Resurrrection of the Author?*, Westport, Conn., Greenwood Press.

——— (2002b) 'Intentionalism and Author Constructs', in William Irwin (ed.) *The Death and Resurrection of the Author?*, Westport, Conn., Greenwood Press, pp. 191–204.

Jacobus, Mary (1986) *Reading Woman: Essays in Feminist Criticism*, London, Methuen.

James, Henry (1981) *Selected Literary Criticism*, ed. Morris Shapiro, Cambridge, Cambridge University Press.

Johnson, Samuel (1963) *'The Idler' and 'The Adventurer'*, ed. W.J. Bate, John M. Bullitt and L.F. Powell, New Haven, Yale University Press.

Joyce, James (2000) *A Portrait of the Artist as a Young Man*, ed. Jeri Johnson, Oxford, Oxford University Press.

Julius, Anthony (1998) 'New Lost Land', *Poetry Review* 88, 1 (Spring): 80–2.

Kamuf, Peggy (1980) 'Writing Like a Woman', in Sally McConnell-Ginet, Ruth Borker and Nelly Furman (eds) *Women and Language in Literature and Society*, New York, Praeger, pp. 284–99.

——— (1988) *Signature Pieces: On the Institution of Authorship*, Ithaca, Cornell University Press.

——— (2002) '"Fiction" and the Experience of the Other', Elizabeth Beaumont Bissell (ed.) *The Question of Literature: The Place of the Literary in Contemporary Theory*, Manchester, Manchester University Press, pp. 156–73.

Kant, Immanuel (1952) *The Critique of Judgement*, trans. James Creed Meredith, Oxford, Clarendon Press.

Keats, John (1958) *The Letters of John Keats*, ed. Hyder Edward Rollins, Cambridge, Mass., Harvard University Press.

Kernan, Alvin (1987) *Printing Technology, Letters and Samuel Johnson*, Princeton, Princeton University Press.

Kerrigan, John (1986), 'Introduction' to William Shakespeare, *The Sonnets and A Lover's Complaint*, ed. John Kerrigan, London, Penguin.

Kewes, Paulina (1998) *Authorship and Appropriation: Writing for the Stage in England 1660–1710*, Oxford, Clarendon Press.

Kimmelman, Burt (1999) *The Poetics of Authorship in the Later Middle Ages: The Emergence of the Modern Literary Persona*, New York, Peter Lang.

Knapp, Steven (1993) *Literary Interest: The Limits of Anti-Formalism*, Cambridge, Mass., Harvard University Press.

Knapp, Steven and Walter Benn Michaels (1985) 'Against Theory', in W.J.T. Mitchell (ed.) *Against Theory: Literary Studies and the New Pragmatism*, Chicago, University of Chicago Press, pp. 11–30.

Knights, L.C. (1946) *Explorations: Essays in Criticism Mainly on the Literature of the Seventeenth Century*, London, Chatto and Windus.

Koestenbaum, Wayne C. (1989) *Double Talk: The Erotics of Male Literary Collaboration*, New York, Routledge.

Kugel, James L. (ed.) (1990) *Poetry and Prophecy: The Beginnings of a Literary Tradition*, Ithaca, Cornell University Press.

Kurke, Leslie (2000) 'The Strangeness of "Song Culture": Archaic Greek Poetry', in Oliver Taplin (ed.) *Literature and the Greek World*, Oxford, Oxford University Press, pp. 40–69.

Lamarque, Peter (2002) 'The Death of the Author: An Analytical Autopsy', in William Irwin (ed.) *The Death and Resurrection of the Author?*, Westport, Conn., Greenwood Press, pp. 79–91.

Leader, Zachary (1996) *Revision and Romantic Authorship*, Oxford, Oxford University Press.

Leitch, Vincent B. (ed.) (2001) *The Norton Anthology of Theory and Criticism*, New York, Norton.

Lerer, Seth (1993) *Chaucer and His Readers: Imagining the Author in Late-Medieval England*, Princeton, Princeton University Press.

Levinson, Jerrold (ed.) (2003) *The Oxford Handbook of Aesthetics*, Oxford, Oxford University Press.

Lipking, Lawrence (1981) *The Life of the Poet: Beginning and Ending Poetic Careers*, Chicago, University of Chicago Press.

—— (1998) 'The Birth of the Author', in Warwick Gould and Thomas F. Stanley (eds) *Writing the Lives of Writers*, Basingstoke, Macmillan, pp. 36–53.

Livingston, Paisley (2003) 'Intention in Art', in Jerrold Levinson (ed.) *The Oxford Handbook of Aesthetics*, Oxford, Oxford University Press, pp. 275–90.

Locke, John (1975) *An Essay Concerning Human Understanding*, ed. Peter H. Nidditch, Oxford, Clarendon Press.

Loewenstein, Joseph (2002a) *The Author's Due: Printing and the Prehistory of Copyright*, Chicago, University of Chicago Press.

—— (2002b) *Ben Johnson and Possessive Authorship*, Cambridge, Cambridge University Press.

Longley, Edna (1998) 'Obfuscating Myths', *Thumbscrew* 10: 27–30.

Lord, Albert B. (1960) *The Singer of Tales*, Cambridge, Mass., Harvard University Press.

Love, Harold (2002) *Attributing Authorship: An Introduction*, Cambridge, Cambridge University Press.

Lowell, Robert (2000) 'On "Skunk Hour"', in W.N. Herbert and Matthew Hollis (eds) *Strong Words: Modern Poets on Modern Poetry*, Tarset, Northumberland, Bloodaxe Books, pp. 106–9.

MacCabe, Colin (2003) 'The Revenge of the Author', in Virginia Wright Wexman (ed.) *Film and Authorship*, New Brunswick, Rutgers University Press, pp. 30–41.

Macherey, Pierre (1995) 'Creation and Production', in Seán Burke (ed.) *Authorship: From Plato to Postmodernism: A Reader.* Edinburgh, Edinburgh University Press, pp. 230–2.

Marotti, Arthur F. (1986) *John Donne, Coterie Poet*, Madison, University of Wisconsin Press.

—— (1995) *Manuscript, Print, and the English Renaissance Lyric*, Ithaca, Cornell University Press.

Martz, Louis L. and Aubrey Williams (eds) (1978) *The Author in His Work: Essays on a Problem in Criticism*, New Haven, Yale University Press.

Masten, Jeffrey (1997) *Textual Intercourse: Collaboration, Authorship, and Sexualities in Renaissance Drama*, Cambridge, Cambridge University Press.

Meltzer, Françoise (1994) *Hot Property: The Stakes and Claims of Literary Originality*, Chicago, University of Chicago Press.

Metz, Walter (2003) 'John Waters Goes to Hollywood: A Poststructuralist Authorship Study', in David A. Gerstner and Janet Staiger (eds) *Authorship and Film*, New York, Routledge, pp. 157–74.

Miller, Edwin Haviland (1959) *The Professional Writer in Elizabethan England: A Study of Nondramatic Literature*, Cambridge, Mass., Harvard University Press.

Miller, Jacqueline T. (1986) *Poetic License: Authority and Authorship in Medieval and Renaissance Contexts*, New York, Oxford University Press.

Miller, Karl (1989) *Authors*, Oxford, Clarendon Press.

Miller, Nancy K. (1995) 'Changing the Subject: Authorship, Writing and the Reader', in Seán Burke (ed.) *Authorship: From Plato to Postmodernism: A Reader*. Edinburgh, Edinburgh University Press, pp. 193–211.

Miller, J. Hillis (2002) *On Literature*, London, Routledge.

Milosz, Czeslaw (1979) 'Ars Poetica?', in Reginald Gibbons (ed.) *The Poet's Work: 29 Poets on the Origins and Practice of Their Art*, Chicago, University of Chicago Press, pp. 3–4.

Minnis, A.J. (1988) *Medieval Theory of Authorship: Scholastic Literary Attitudes in the Later Middle Ages*, 2nd edn, Aldershot, Scolar.

Moi, Toril (1985) *Sexual/Textual Politics: Feminist Literary Theory*, London, Methuen.

Montrose, Louis (1998) 'Professing the Renaissance: The Poetics and Politics of Culture', in Julie Rivkin and Michael Ryan (eds) *Literary Theory: An Anthology*, Oxford, Blackwell, pp. 777–85.

Morgan, Michael (1988) 'Authorship and the History of Philosophy', *Review of Metaphysics* 42: 327–55.

Moriarty, Michael (1991) *Roland Barthes*, Cambridge, Polity.

Motion, Andrew (1998) 'A Thunderbolt from the Blue: This Book will Live Forever', *The Times* (17 January): 22.

Murray, Penelope (1989) 'Poetic Genius and its Classical Origins', in Penelope Murray (ed.) *Genius: The History of an Idea*, Oxford, Basil Blackwell, pp. 9–31.

Nagy, Gregory (1989) 'Early Greek Views of Poets and Poetry', in George A. Kennedy (ed.) *The Cambridge History of Literary Criticism*, vol. 1: *Classical Criticism*, Cambridge, Cambridge University Press, pp. 1–77.

—— (1996a) *Homeric Questions*, Austin, University of Texas Press.

—— (1996b) *Poetry as Performance: Homer and Beyond*, Cambridge, Cambridge University Press.

—— (2003) *Homeric Responses*, Austin, University of Texas Press.

Nehemas, Alexander (1981) 'The Postulated Author: Critical Monism as Regulative Ideal', *Critical Inquiry* 8: 131–49.

—— (1986) 'What an Author Is', *The Journal of Philosophy* 83: 685–91.

—— (2002) 'Writer, Text, Work, Author', in William Irwin (ed.) *The Death and Resurrection of the Author?*, Westport, Conn., Greenwood Press, pp. 95–115.

Nesbit, Molly (1987) 'What Was an Author?', *Yale French Studies* 73: 229–57.

Newlyn, Lucy (2000) *Reading, Writing, and Romanticism: The Anxiety of Reception*, Oxford, Oxford University Press.

North, Michael (2001) 'Authorship and Autography', *PMLA* 116, 5: 1377–85.

North, Marcy L. (2003) *The Anonymous Renaissance: Cultures of Discretion in Tudor-Stuart England*, Chicago, University of Chicago Press.

O'Brien, Sean (2003) 'Essential but Unlovely', *Guardian Review* (1 November): 25.

Olson, David R. (1994) *The World as Paper: The Conceptual and Cognitive Implications of Writing and Reading*, Cambridge, Cambridge University Press.

Ong, Walter (1982) *Orality and Literacy: The Technologizing of the Word*, London, Routledge.

Pask, Kevin (1996) *The Emergence of the English Author: Scripting the Life of the Poet in Early Modern England*, Cambridge, Cambridge University Press.

Patterson, Annabel (1990) 'Intention', in Frank Lentricchia and Thomas McLaughlin (eds) *Critical Terms for Literary Study*, Chicago, University of Chicago Press, pp. 135–46.

Paz, Octavio, Jacques Roubaud, Edoardo Sanguineti and Charles Tomlinson (1971) *Renga: A Chain of Poems*, trans. Charles Tomlinson, New York, George Braziller.

Peacock, Thomas Love (1987) 'The Four Ages of Poetry', in David Bromwich (ed.) *Romantic Critical Essays*, Cambridge, Cambridge University Press.

Pease, Donald E. (1990) 'Author', in Frank Lentricchia and Thomas McLaughlin (eds) *Critical Terms for Literary Study*, Chicago, University of Chicago Press, pp. 105–17.

Pessoa, Fernando (1979) 'Towards Explaining Heteronymy', in Reginald Gibbons (ed.) *The Poet's Work: 29 Poets on the Origins and Practice of Their Art*, Chicago, University of Chicago Press, pp. 5–15.

Plato (2001a) *Ion*, in Vincent B. Leitch (ed.) *The Norton Anthology of Theory and Criticism*, New York, Norton, pp. 37–48.

—— (2001b) *Republic*, in Vincent B. Leitch (ed.) *The Norton Anthology of Theory and Criticism*, New York, Norton, pp. 49–80.

—— (2001c) *Phaedrus*, in Vincent B. Leitch (ed.) *The Norton Anthology of Theory and Criticism*, New York, Norton, pp. 81–5.

Quaint, David (1983) *Origin and Originality in Renaissance Literature*, New Haven, Yale University Press.

Ransom, John Crowe (1968) *The World's Body*, Baton Rouge, Louisiana State University Press.

Rice, Philip and Patricia Waugh (eds) (1996) *Modern Literary Theory: A Reader*, 3rd edn, London, Arnold.

Ridley, Aaron (2003) 'Expression in Art', in Jerrold Levinson (ed.) *The Oxford Handbook of Aesthetics*, Oxford, Oxford University Press, pp. 211–27.

Rintoul, M.C. (1993) *Dictionary of Real People and Places in Fiction*, London, Routledge.

Rivkin, Julie and Michael Ryan (eds) (1998) *Literary Theory: An Anthology*, Oxford, Blackwell.

Rogers, Pat (2002) 'Nameless Names: Pope, Curll, and the Uses of Anonymity', *New Literary History* 33: 233–45.

Rorty, Richard (1995) 'Taking Philosophy Seriously', in Seán Burke (ed.) *Authorship: From Plato to Postmodernism: A Reader*. Edinburgh, Edinburgh University Press, pp. 292–9.

Rose, Mark (1993) *Authors and Owners: The Invention of Copyright*, Cambridge, Mass., Harvard University Press.

Rosebury, Brian (1997) 'Irrecoverable Intentions and Literary Interpretation', *British Journal of Aesthetics* 37: 15–30.

Ross, Marlon B. (1989) *The Contours of Masculine Desire: Romanticism and the Rise of Women's Poetry*, New York, Oxford University Press.

Royle, Nicholas (2003) *Jacques Derrida*, London, Routledge.

Rushdie, Salman (1988) *The Satanic Verses*, Harmondsworth, Viking.

Ruthven, K.K. (2001) *Faking Literature*, Cambridge, Cambridge University Press.

Said, Edward (1983) 'On Originality', in *The World, the Text, and the Critic*, Cambridge, Mass., Harvard University Press, pp. 126–39.

—— (2003) 'A Window on the World', *Guardian Review* (2 August): 4–6.

Salokannel, Marjut (2003) 'Cinema in Search of Its Authors: On the Notion of Film Authorship in Legal Discourse', in Virginia Wright Wexman (ed.) *Film and Authorship*, New Brunswick, Rutgers University Press, pp. 152–78.

Sarris, Andrew (2003) 'The Auteur Theory Revisited', in Virginia Wright Wexman (ed.) *Film and Authorship*, New Brunswick, Rutgers University Press, pp. 21–29.

Saunders, J.W. (1964) *The Profession of English Letters*, London, Routledge and Kegan Paul.

Saunders, David (1992) *Authorship and Copyright*, London, Routledge.

Saunders, David and Ian Hunter (1991) 'Lessons from the "Literary": How to Historicise Authorship', *Critical Inquiry* 17: 479–509.

Schatz, Thomas (2003) 'The Whole Equation of Pictures', in Virginia Wright Wexman (ed.) *Film and Authorship*, New Brunswick, Rutgers University Press, pp. 89–95.

Schiller, Friedrich (1988) extract from *On Naïve and Sentimental Poetry*, in David Simpson (ed.) *The Origin of Modern Critical Thought: German Aesthetic and Literary Criticism from Lessing to Hegel*, Cambridge, Cambridge University Press.

Shelley, Percy Bysshe (1977) *Shelley's Poetry and Prose*, ed. Donald H. Reiman and Sharon B. Powers, New York, Norton.

Sherman, Brad and Alain Strowel (eds) (1994) *Of Authors and Origins: Essays on Copyright Law*, Oxford, Clarendon Press.

Showalter, Elaine (1986) 'Feminist Criticism in the Wilderness', in Elaine Showalter (ed.) *The New Feminist Criticism: Essays on Women, Literature, and Theory*, London, Virago, pp. 243–70.

Sidney, Sir Philip (2002) *An Apology for Poetry (or The Defence of Poesy)*, ed. Geoffrey

Shepherd, 3rd edn, revised by R.W. Meslen, Manchester, Manchester University Press.

Siskin, Clifford (1998) *The Work of Writing: Literature and Social Change in Britain, 1700–1830*, Baltimore, Johns Hopkins University Press.

Staiger, Janet (2003) 'Authorship Approaches', in David A. Gerstner and Janet Staiger (eds) *Authorship and Film*, New York, Routledge, pp. 27–57.

Stallybrass, Peter and Allon White (1986) *The Politics and Poetics of Transgression*, London, Methuen.

Stecker, Robert (1987) 'Apparent, Implied, and Postulated Authors', *Philosophy and Literature* 11: 255–71.

Stevens, Wallace (1960) 'The Noble Rider and the Sound of Words', in *The Necessary Angel: Essays on Reality and the Imagination*, London, Faber and Faber, pp. 3–36.

—— (1979) 'The Irrational Element in Poetry', in Reginald Gibbons (ed.) *The Poet's Work: 29 Poets on the Origins and Practice of Their Art*, Chicago, University of Chicago Press, pp. 48–58.

Stewart, Susan (1991) *Crimes of Writing: Problems in the Containment of Representation*, New York, Oxford University Press.

Stillinger, Jack (1991) *Multiple Authorship and the Myth of the Solitary Genius*, Oxford, Oxford University Press.

Summit, Jennifer (2000) *Lost Property: The Woman Writer and English Literary History, 1380–1589*, Chicago, Chicago University Press.

Swinden, Patrick (1999) *Literature and the Philosophy of Intention*, London, Macmillan.

Taplin, Oliver (2000a) 'Introduction', in Oliver Taplin (ed.) *Literature in the Greek World*, Oxford, Oxford University Press, pp. xv–xxvii.

—— (2000b) 'The Spring of the Muses: Homer and Related Poetry' in Oliver Taplin (ed.) *Literature in the Greek World*, Oxford, Oxford University Press, pp. 4–39.

Taylor, Charles (1989) *Sources of the Self: The Making of the Modern Identity*, Cambridge, Cambridge University Press.

Todd, Janet (1989) *The Sign of Angellica: Women, Writing, and Fiction 1660–1800*, London, Virago.

Tomaschevsky, Boris (1971) 'Literature and Biography', in Ladislav Matejka and Krystyna Pomorska (eds) *Readings in Russian Poetics: Formalist and Structuralist Views*, Cambridge, Mass., MIT Press, pp. 47–55.

Trigg, Stephanie (2002) *Congenial Souls: Reading Chaucer from Medieval to Postmodern*, Minneapolis, University of Minnesota Press.

Turner, Cheryl (1992) *Living by the Pen: Women Writers in the Eighteenth Century*, London, Routledge.

Vickers, Brian (ed.) (1999) *English Renaissance Literary Criticism*, Oxford, Clarendon Press.

—— (2002a) *Shakespeare, Co-Author: A Historical Study of Five Collaborative Plays*, Oxford, Oxford University Press.

—— (2002b) 'Counterfeiting' Shakespeare: Evidence, Authorship, and John Ford's 'A Funerall Elegye', Cambridge, Cambridge University Press.

Wall, Wendy (1993) The Imprint of Gender: Authorship and Publication in the English Renaissance, Ithaca, Cornell University Press.

Walsh, Thomas R. and Rodney Merrill (2002) 'The Odyssey: The Tradition, the Singer, the Performance', in Homer, The Odyssey, trans. Rodney Merrill, Ann Arbor, University of Michigan Press, pp. 1–53.

Weberman, David (2002) 'Gadamer's Hermeneutics and the Question of Authorial Intention', in William Irwin (ed.) The Death and Resurrection of the Author?, Westport, Conn., Greenwood Press, pp. 45–64.

Wexman, Virginia Wright (ed.) (2003) Film and Authorship, New Brunswick, Rutgers University Press.

Williams, Raymond (1988) Keywords: A Vocabulary of Culture and Society, revised edn, London, Fontana.

Wimsatt, W.K. (1954) The Verbal Icon: Studies in the Meaning of Poetry, Lexington, University of Kentucky Press.

—— (1976) 'Genesis: A Fallacy Revisited', in David Newton de Molina (ed.) On Literary Intention, Edinburgh, Edinburgh University Press, pp. 116–38.

Wimsatt, W.K. and Beardsley, Monroe C. (1954) 'The Intentional Fallacy', in W.K. Wimsatt, The Verbal Icon: Studies in the Meaning of Poetry, Lexington, University of Kentucky Press, pp. 3–18.

Wogan-Browne, Jocelyn, Nicholas Watson, Andrew Taylor and Ruth Evans (eds) (1999) The Idea of the Vernacular: An Anthology of Middle English Literary Theory, 1280–1520, Exeter, Exeter University Press.

Wollen, Peter (1981) 'The Auteur Theory', in John Caughie (ed.) Theories of Authorship: A Reader, London, Routledge and Kegan Paul, pp. 138–51.

—— (2003) 'The Auteur Theory: Michael Curtz, and Casablanca', in David A. Gerstner and Janet Staiger (eds) Authorship and Film, New York, Routledge, pp. 61–76.

Wood, Michael (1994) The Magician's Doubts: Nabakov and the Risks of Fiction, London, Chatto and Windus.

Woodmansee, Martha (1994a) The Author, Art, and the Market: Rereading the History of Aesthetics, New York, Columbia University Press.

—— (1994b) 'On the Author Effect: Recovering Collectivity', in Martha Woodmansee and Peter Jaszi (eds) The Construction of Authorship: Textual Appropriation in Law and Literature, Durham, NC, Duke University Press, pp. 15–28.

Woodmansee, Martha and Peter Jaszi (eds) (1994) The Construction of Authorship: Textual Appropriation in Law and Literature, Durham, NC, Duke University Press.

Wordsworth, William (1984) The Oxford Authors William Wordsworth, ed. Stephen Gill, Oxford, Oxford University Press.

Yeats, W.B. (1994) Later Essays, ed. William H. O'Donnell, New York, Charles Scribner's Sons.

Young, Edward (1918) Conjectures on Original Composition, ed. Edith J. Morley, Manchester, Manchester University Press.

INDEX